Traditions
Past and Present

by
Joanna Hubbard

the Peppertree Press
Sarasota, Florida

For information regarding permission,
call 941-922-2662 or contact us at our website:
www.peppertreepublishing.com or write to:
the Peppertree Press, LLC.
Attention: Publisher
1269 First Street, Suite 7
Sarasota, Florida 34236

ISBN: 978-1-61493-447-9

Library of Congress Number: 2016914912

Printed September 2016

DEDICATION

I just want to thank both of my parents,
Olie and Shirley Hubbard,
for giving me birth in Henryville, Indiana
and training me in the sight of God.
I thank God for inspiring me to write this book.
I thank God for my three sons:
Chandler, Micheal, and David.

Table of Contents

CHAPTER 1 - HISTORY OF CHRISTMAS   1
The Myth of Christmas   1
Santa Claus Comes from Saint Nicholas   3
In the Eyes of Children   8
"God wants us to open our minds."   11
Syncretism   12
Paganism Blended into the Church   12
How Did Christmas Come to Be
Celebrated on December 25th?   16
The Earliest Christmas   18
The Roots of the Christmas Tree   19
The Source of Holly Wreaths, Yule Logs, and Mistletoe   22
The Roots of Mistletoe   23
When Was Jesus Born?   24
What Does God Say about Christians
Who Practice Pagan Customs?   27

CHAPTER 2 – NEW YEAR'S   29
History   29
New Year's Eve by the Numbers   30

CHAPTER 3 – LEAP YEAR   34
History   34

CHAPTER 4 – APRIL FOOLS' DAY   36
All Fools' Day   36
Earlier Celebrations   37
April Fools' Day Tricks   37

CHAPTER 5 – ST. PATRICK'S DAY   39
Religious Feast Day   39
Was St. Patrick Irish?   39
Leprechauns   42
On St. Patrick's Day, Why Do People Wear Green?   44

CHAPTER 6 – EASTER   45
Is Easter Biblical?   45

CHAPTER 7 – MOTHER'S DAY 47
U.S. History 47
Founding 47
Mothering Sunday 49
Early History of Mother's Day 53
The Goddess, Rhea, Wife of Cronus 54

CHAPTER 8 – FATHER'S DAY 57

CHAPTER 9 – THANKSGIVING DAY 62
The First Thanksgiving 62
Thanksgiving Dinner for the Pilgrims 65
Squanto 65
Etymology 66

CHAPTER 10 – HALLOWEEN 67
Pagan vs. Christian Celebrations 67
Celebrating Halloween 68

CHAPTER 11 – YOM KIPPER 71

**CHAPTER 12 – FAMOUS JEWISH PEOPLE
            WHO WROTE HOLIDAY SONGS** 73
Celebrating the Holidays with Song 73

CHAPTER 13 —VALENTINE'S DAY 77
Juno Februata 78
Cupid 79
The Heart Symbol 79
Valentine's Day by the Numbers 80
Flowers Symbols 83

CHAPTER 14 —BIRTHDAYS 84
Biblical Background 84

CHAPTER 15 —JEWISH HOLIDAYS 89
Astronomical Phenomenas 89
Months of the Jewish Calendar 95
God's Law and Time vs. Man 97
Keeping Track of the Sabbath 101
The Manna Miracle 104

CHRISTMAS

LINLEY SAMBOURNE DEL.

History of Christmas

The Myth of Christmas

Parents reason that they owe the whole Christmas myth to their children. Christmas traditions are focused primarily on kids, and they are certainly the center of most of what happens. I know, because I kept them until I was in the fourth grade. My oldest brother and younger sister and I were the recipients of much and the givers of very little on Christmas Eve—and especially Christmas day—and it all started with the Santa Claus lie.

When I was in the fifth grade, I told my teacher at school that Santa was a lie, and I wasn't allowed to partake of the decorating of the classroom. I was ushered out of my class down to the principal's office. The only time students were allowed to go to the principal's office back in those days is when someone did a bad deed or to pick up supplies. I knew I didn't do anything bad, nor was I going there to pick up supplies.

I spent most of my school years unhappy and miserable. My parents had found this minister on the radio in the 1960s preaching the truth—our household was just one of the hundreds that heard and read his literature, and traveled to different churches in Indiana and Ohio, to learn more of this new truth that was sweeping like a wildfire across the world. A few of my classmates had overheard me when I told my teacher, "Satan is alive …" Some of them started crying—even boys!

At my young age, what in the world did I do wrong? From one school year to the next, they seem to look at me with disapproval. On that day, in that year, I had "killed Santa!" When I was allowed back into the classroom at the end of day, it was pretty with all the trimmings of green and red paper mache glued together and hooked to a string from one end of the room to the next.

Everyone had a red stocking hung up on the pegs for Santa to drop goodies into the bag for children to take home for Christmas break. Everyone had one, except me. No candy or nuts in my bag. I remember seeing the wreath that they had made out of paper, spray-painted green, and decorated. They even made a Christmas tree out of little magazines and spray-painted and decorated them as well. And then, they even colored a picture of Santa with his reindeers and a sleigh. I remember the same thing nearly happened to me a couple of years before, when I told the truth about the Easter bunny being a lie.

During my school years, I caused chaos, because of my parent's new religious beliefs. I spent many days either in the principal's office or out in the hallway writing dictionary pages, only because I never knew how to keep my mouth shut and not to rebel against my teachers for telling the truth—that was my crime!

Back home in the small community where I grew up in southern Indiana, there were three churches. My teachers tried to convince me at least one or two of those preachers from other churches should know if Easter or Christmas was the truth or not. So I remember seeing a priest and another man showing up and giving a message on those two topics. At that point, I was confused, because I thought as a child, but I remembered what my parents had taught me as well—thou shall not lie, according to God.

> "Santa," was a common name for Nimrod Minor throughout Asia Minor. This is also the same fire god who came down the chimneys of the ancient pagans and to whom infants were burned and eaten in human sacrifice among those who were once God's people.

Langer, William, L. "Santa." An Encyclopedia of World History, 5th revised edition. Boston, MA: Houghton Mifflin, 1968, and 1972

Santa Claus Comes from Saint Nicholas

Nicholas was born in Parara, Turkey in 270 C.E and later because Bishop of Myra. He died in 345 C.E. on December 6th, but he was only named a saint in the 19th century. Nicholas was among the most senior bishops who convened the Council of Nicaea in 325 C.E. and created the New Testament as we know it presently ("AND MYSELF!"). The text they produced portrayed the Jews as the "children of the devil"—who sentenced Jews to death?

In 1087, a group of sailor who idolized Nicholas moved his bones from turkey to a sanctuary in Bari, Italy. There, Nicholas supplanted a female deity called "the Grandmother," or "Pasqua Epiphania," who used to fill the children's stockings with her gifts. The grandmother was ousted from her shrine at Bari, which became the center of Nicholas cult.

Members of this group gave each other gifts during a pageant they conducted annually on the anniversary of Nicholas' death, December 6th. The Nicholas cult spread north until it was adopted by the Germans and Celtic pagans. These groups worshipped a pantheon led by Woden—their chief god and father of Thor, Balder, and Tin. Woden had a long white beard and rode a horse through the heavens one evening each autumn. When Nicholas merged with Woden, he shed his Mediterranean appearance—grew a beard, mounted a flying horse, rescheduled his flight for later in December, and donned heavy winter clothing. In a bid for pagan adherents in northern Europe, the Catholic

Church adopted the Nicholas cult and taught that he did (and they should) distribute gifts on December 25th instead of December 6th.

In 1809, the novelist Washington Irving (most famous for his story called *The Legend of Sleepy Hollow* and that of Rip Van Winkle), wrote a satire of Dutch culture entitled *Knickerbocker History*. The satire refers several times to the white-bearded Saint Nicholas riding a flying horse using his Dutch name, Santa Claus, who is also known as "jolly St. Nick." I have heard some preachers refer to "old Nick" as a term for the devil. Have you ever noticed that Santa and Satan is an anagram? Perhaps it is because Satan is the father of all lies and Santa is a lie made up from Satan.

Most people never take the time to reflect on why they believe, or what they believe, or do what they should do. Generally, they accept common religious practices without question, choosing to do what everyone else is doing because it feels good to go along with the crowd of the world. Most follow along as they go from one generation to the next, assuming that what they believe and are taught, even by men and women wearing the robe and neckband, is right.

They take their beliefs for granted to be the truth and never take time to study the Word of God for themselves to look for the proof. Nowhere is this truer than the observance of Christmas. Most people even profess Christmas is "found in the Bible." Surely hundreds of billions of people cannot be wrong. Or can they? Let's turn in our Bibles to Mark 7:6-9:

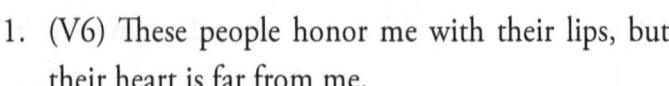

1. (V6) These people honor me with their lips, but their heart is far from me.
2. (V7) And in vain they worship me, teaching in doctrines the commandments of men.
3. (V8) For laying aside the commandments of God, you hold the tradition of men,
4. (V9) All too well you reject the commandments of God, that you may keep your traditions.

Clement Moore, a professor at a union seminary had published a poem he wrote based on the character of Santa Claus: "Twas the night before Christmas, and all through the house, not a creature was stirring, not even a mouse! The stockings were hung by the chimney with care, in hopes that St. Nicholas soon would be there ..." Moore innovated by portraying a Santa with eight reindeer who descended through chimneys.

The Bavarian illustrator, Thomas Nast, almost completed the modern picture of Santa Claus. From 1862 through 1886 based on Moore's poem, Nast drew more than 2,200 cartoon images of Santa for Harpers Weekly. Before Nast, Saint Nicholas had been pictured as everything from a stern-looking bishop to a gnome-type figure in a frock. Nast also gave Santa a home at the North Pole, his workshop filled with elves, and his list of the good and bad little boys and girls around the world. All Santa was missing was his red outfit.

In 1931, the Coca Cola Corporation contracted the

Swedish commercial artist, Haddon Sundblum, to create a Coke-drinking Santa. Sundblum modeled his Santa on his friend, Lou Prentice—chosen for his cheerful, chubby face. The Coca Cola Corporation insisted that Santa's fur-trimmed suit be bright, and Coca Cola "red." And Santa Claus was born—a gamut of Christian crusader, pagan god, and of course, a commercial idol.

Santa Claus is a modern incarnation of the most depraved pagan rituals ever practiced on earth. Many professing Christians around the world who are excitedly preparing for their Christmas celebrations would not prefer the holiday's real significance. If they do know the history, they often object that celebration has nothing to do with the holiday's monstrous history and meaning—it's for the kids! "And it's perfect innocent fun!"

Let's look at this example—consider that between 1933-1945, the Nazi regime celebrated Adolf Hitler's birthday on April 20th as a holiday. Imagine that they named the day, "Hitler Day," and observed the day with feasting, drunkenness, gift-giving, running naked in the streets, sexual indulgence, and various pagan practices. Imagine that on that day, Jews were historically subjected to perverse torture and abuse that languished for centuries.

Now, imagine that your great-great-grandchildren were about to celebrate "Hitler Day"—April 20th has arrived. They had long forgotten about Auschwitz and Bergen-Belson. They had never heard of gas chambers and death marches. They had purchased champagne and caviar, and were about to begin the party when someone reminded them of the day's real history and their ancestors agony. Imagine that they initially objected, "We aren't celebrating the holocaust. We're just having a little Hitler Day party." If you could travel forward in time and meet them and say a few words, what would you advise them to do on Hitler Day?

On December 25th, 1941, Julius Stricher, one of Hitler's assistants, celebrated Christmas by penning the following editorial in his rabidly anti-Semitic newspaper, *Der Stuermer*: "If one really wants to put an end to the continuing prospering of this curse from heaven that is the Jewish blood, there is only one way to do it: to eradicate this people, this Satan's son, root and branch." It was an appropriate thought for this Christmas Day, so how will we celebrate?

Lawrence Kelemen. http://www.simpletoremember.com/vitals/ Christmas_TheRealStory.htm

In the Eyes of Children

A few years ago, I was ringing a bell for a famous religious organization, who helps supply food, clothing, toys, shelter, and outreach programs encompassing people needing help. As I was standing there ringing the bell, a little girl first approached the kettle with her piggy bank: she then emptied all of her savings into the pot. She told me that it is better to give than to receive. She wanted to help baby

Jesus help other people in need. As she continued to empty her piggybank, a woman strolled up to the pot to add a dollar into the contribution. She stated to the young girl, "Oh, Santa knows what you are doing, and that makes you a good little girl." To my surprise the little girl replied while facing the older woman, "I don't believe in Santa, but I do believe in Jesus!" Then, I had to smile at her and her father standing by, because he was training his child in God's way.

You will search each store until you are exhausted. There will be shoppers everywhere, pushing and shoving just to stay in line for hours to purchase the "right" gifts. You will be willing to shop everywhere—malls, department stores, and yard sales, flea markets, e-Bay, and Amazon. This will represent a tremendous amount of patience's in order to buy gifts.

- Losing sleep
- Headaches
- Tired feet
- Hungry
- Madness
- Car parking

- Standing in lines
- Looking for a seat to crash on
- Credit card debts/being broke until next payday
- Once again for the 100th time sitting on Santa's lap
- Listening to Christmas carols
- Being mugged by a thief

Then you have to put up with their whining. You are trying to please everyone, children, friends, loved ones, neighbors, your dog, making sure that everyone who had their names on the list got a gift. All this just to please your child or someone else. What about yourself?

Most people today believe that gift giving comes from the Word of God. But does it? Where is your proof? The bibliotheca sacra states:

> "The interchange of presents between friends is a characteristic of Christmas and the Saturnalia, and must have been adopted by Christians from the pagans, as the admonition of Tertullian plainly shows" (Vol 12, pp 153-155).

Like every other aspect of Christmas, the shocking truth is that even this supposedly Christian custom does not come from the Bible. It is ironical that people love to believe they are following the customs of the wise men giving to Christ, when actually they are giving almost exclusively to each other. In fact, most people give to others on Christmas merely because they expect to receive gifts themselves.

"God wants us to open our minds."

The majority of people will stoutly defend what they have merely assumed is right or biblical. They will read with prejudice anything that contradicts their assumptions, when you read this book, I ask God to guide you—to help you prove what He says in the Word of God. 2 Tim. 3:16 says:

> All scriptures are given by inspiration of god and are profitable for doctrine, for reproof, for correction, for instruction in righteousness.

In other words, for all who are willing to accept it—for all who truly want to serve and please God, who is the author of the Bible. He does not want anyone to be confused. He commands us to study. Please read the Scriptures: 2 Tim. 2:15; Matt. 4:4; Duet. 8:3; Rom. 6:16-23; Rom. 12:2; Is. 66:2.

Today the ministers of this world have utterly failed in their responsibility to teach the nations of the world God's precious Word. They have stood up on platforms to deceive and delude the masses of God's people with false practice and gross misunderstanding. God wants everyone to understand His Word. It is not just for ministers, theologians, and religionists. God wants the meek to know His Word. He will even call ones who have no education at all to do His work, if they are willing to listen and obey the call of His voice.

Syncretism

The modern term for merging false pagan customs with the worship of the true God is called Syncretism. In Biblical days, ancient Israel's God had put Jews to death—it was that serious (Lev. 18:29). When Israel thought and believed, in their own minds, they worshiped God as an entire nation, comes from 2 Kings 17:33:

> They feared the Lord, and served their own gods, after the manner of the nations whom they carried away from there.

If true, did you grasp it? They had feared God, and yet served their own god. Yet in verse 34, it states that they never truly feared the true God. This is how God views what people are doing today—no matter what these people copying ancient pagan practices might think of their own actions!

Please read these Scriptures, Duet 12:32; Lev. 20: 22-26; Duet. 20: 13-18; Ex. 34:10-7; Ex. 23:23-23.

Paganism Blended into the Church

Here is another source, which demonstrates how this all came to be a heritage practiced so "innocently" by billions around the world—yet far from innocent in God's sight.

> "Christianity ... by a complex and gradual process ... became the official religion of the Roman Empire."
> "For a time, coins and other monuments continued to

link Christian doctrines with worship of the sun, which Constantine had been addicted previously, but even when this phase came to an end, Roman paganism continued to exert other permanent influences, great and small. The ecclesiastical calendar retains numerous remnants of pre-Christian festivals, notably Christmas, which blends elements that includes of both the feast of the Saturnalia and the birthday of Mithra. But most of all, the mainstream of western Christianity owed ancient Rome the firm disciple that gave it stability and shape.

The Encyclopedia Britannia 15th Ed, Vol. 10, Pgs. 1062-3;

The new *Schaff-Herzog Encyclopedia of Religious Knowledge* teaches us how this powerful ideation, this pagan festival slipped into the "Christian" world, under "Christmas."

"How much the date of the festival depended upon the pagan Brumalia (Dec 25th) following the Saturnalia (Dec 24th), and celebrating the shortest days of the years, and the 'new sun' ... cannot be set aside by Christian influence ... The pagan festival with its riot and merry-making was so popular that Christians were glad of an excuse to continue its celebrations with little change in spirit and in manner. Christian preachers of the West and the Near East protested against the unseeingly frivolity with which Christ's birthday was celebrated, while Christians of Mesopotamia accused their western brethren of idolatry and sun worship for adopting as Christian this pagan festival."

Here is one additional source to reveal how the Roman Church absorbed Christmas into an official celebration. *The Encyclopedia Britannica,* 1945 ed. states:

> "Christmas was not among the earliest festivals of the church ... Certain Latins, as early as 354, may have transferred the birthday from January 6th to December 25th, which was then a Mithraic Feast ... or birthday of the unconquered sun ... The Syrians and Armenians, who clung to January 6th, accused the Romans of sun worship and idolatry, contending that the feast of December 25th had been invented by disciples of Cerin, thus ... celebrated long before Christ's birth found its way into recognized Christianity."

Did you know, during the 17th century, the Puritans of New England understood how wrong Christmas was? They actually banned its observance by law in 1659, throughout the Massachusetts Bay colony. Fines and imprisonment could result from being found keeping it. The Puritans knew its roots and labeled it, "heathen papist idolatry."

On December 25, 1884, Christian leaders whipped the Polish masses into anti-Semitic frenzies that led to riots across the country. In Warsaw, 12 Jews were brutally murdered, Jewish women were raped, and two million rubles destroyed.

In Rev. 2:6-15, Jesus talks to John about the loveless church:

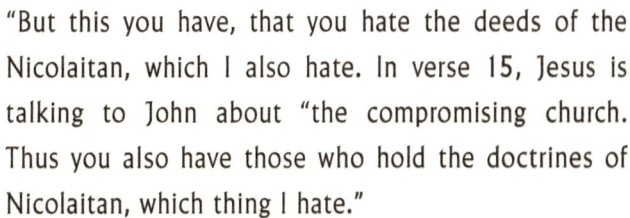

"But this you have, that you hate the deeds of the Nicolaitan, which I also hate. In verse 15, Jesus is talking to John about "the compromising church. Thus you also have those who hold the doctrines of Nicolaitan, which thing I hate."

Notice my readers, Jesus twice tells the church, not once, but twice that (he) hates. Let's analyze the word, "Nicolaitan." It means "followers of the Nicolas." Nikos means "conquerors or destroyer." Laos means "people." Nicolaitan, then, are people who follow the conquerors or destroyer Nimrod.

Consider this my readers, following Christmas as an innocent Christian custom is very dangerous, according to the Word of God. And if he hates it, should not true professing Christians hate it as well?

There is no Christian church with a tradition that Jesus was really born on December 25th. This is a day on which Jews have been shamed, tortured, and murdered.

Consider these quotes from the *Catholic Encyclopedia*, 1911 Ed., under "Christmas." Christmas was not among the earliest festivals of the church ... the first evidence of the feast is from Egypt. "Further, pagan customs centering on the January calendar gravitated to Christmas." Under "natal days," origin, an early catholic rite, admitted, "In the Scriptures, no one is recorded to have kept a feast or held a great banquet on his birthday." The 1956 edition adds, "Christmas was not observed in the first centuries of the Christian church, since the Christian usage in general was to celebrate the death of remarkable persons rather than their birth ... a feast was established in memory of this event (Christ's birth) in the 4th century."

In the 5th century, the western church ordered the feast to be celebrated on the day of the Mithraic rites of the birth of the sun and at the close of the Saturnalia festival, as no certain knowledge of the day of Christ's birth existed."

It was 300 years after Christ died before the Roman Church kept Christmas, and not until the 5th century that it was mandated to be kept throughout the empire as an official festival honoring Christ. Anyone who refused was put to death. God plainly says, "Do not follow the way of the heathens. In modern times, we are no different than the people before us. We say we love God with all our heart, soul, and mind, but when God asks us to put away the pagan ways, we would rather cling to them, thus not obeying His voice, and losing our soul, instead of spending a lifetime of eternal life here on earth with him in His Kingdom yet to come.

How Did Christmas Come to Be Celebrated on December 25th?

Roman pagans first introduced the holiday of Saturnalia, a weeklong period of lawlessness, celebrated between December 17th through 25th. During this period, Roman courts were closed, and Roman law dictated that no one could be punished for damaging property or injuring

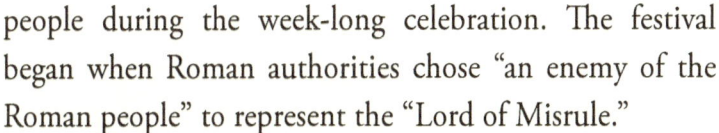

people during the week-long celebration. The festival began when Roman authorities chose "an enemy of the Roman people" to represent the "Lord of Misrule."

Each Roman community selected a victim whom they forced to indulge in food and other physical pleasures throughout the week. At the festival's conclusion, December 25th, Roman authorities believed they were destroying the forces of darkness by brutally murdering innocent men and women. The ancient Greek writer, poet, and historian, Lucian (in his dialogue entitled *Saturnalia*), describes the festival's observance in his time. In addition to human sacrifice, he mentions these customs: widespread intoxication; going house-to-house singing naked; rape and other sexual license; and consuming human-shaped biscuits (still produced in some English and German bakeries during the Christmas season).

In the 4th century CE, Christianity imported the Saturnalia festival, hoping to take the pagan masses in with it. Christian leaders succeeded in converting to Christianity large numbers of pagans by promising them that they could continue to celebrate the Saturnalia as Christians. The problem was that there was nothing intrinsically Christian about Saturnalia.

Remember this—these Christian leaders named Saturnalia's concluding day, Dec. 25th, to be Jesus" birthday. Christians had little success, however, refining the practices of Saturnalia. As Stephen Nissenbaum, professor of history at the University of Massachusetts Amherst writes:

" ... in return for ensuring massive observance of the anniversary of the Savior's birth by assigning it to this renaissance date, the church for its part tacitly agreed to be celebrated more or less the way it had always been."

The Earliest Christmas

The earliest Christmas holidays were celebrated by drinking, sexual indulgence, singing naked in the streets (a precursor of modern caroling), etc. The Reverend Increase Mather of Boston observed in 1687 that "the early Christians who first observed the nativity on Dec 25th did not do so thinking that Christ was born in that month, but because the heathens' Saturnalia was at that time kept in Rome, and they were willing to have those pagan holidays metamorphosed into Christians ones."

Because of its known pagan origins, Christmas was banned by the Puritans and its observance was illegal in Massachusetts in 1659-1681. However, Christmas was and still is celebrated by most Christians. Some of the most depraved customs of the Saturnalia carnival were intentionally revived by the Catholic Church in 1466 when Pope Paul II, for the amusement of his Roman citizens, forced Jews to race naked through the streets of the city. An eyewitness count reports, "Before they feed richly, as to make the race more difficult for them and at the same time more amusing for spectators."

They ran ... amid Rome's taunting shrieks and peals of laughter, while the Holy Father stood upon a richly ornamental balcony and laughed heartily. As part of the Saturnalia carnival throughout the 18th and 19th centuries C.E., rabbis of the ghetto in Rome were forced to wear clownish outfits and march throughout the city streets to the jeers of the crowd, petted by a variety of misers. When the Jewish community of Rome sent a petition in 1836 to Pope Gregory XVI begging him to stop the annual Saturnalia abuse of the Jewish community, he refused to listen to their pleas.

The Christmas challenge has always been a holiday celebrated carelessly. For millennia, pagans, Christians, and even Jews have been swept away in the season's festivities and very few people even paused to consider the celebration's intrinsic meaning or history of surroundings.

The Roots of the Christmas Tree

No book about Christmas is complete without some explanation of the "Christmas tree." We have touched on it without directly focusing on it. The modern Christmas tree originated in Germany, but the Germans got it from the Romans, who got it from the Babylonians and Egyptians. The following quote demonstrates what the Babylonians believed about the root of the Christmas tree:

"... an old Babylon's fable told of an evergreen tree which sprang to life out of a dead tree stump. The old stump symbolized the dead Nimrod, The new evergreen tree symbolized that Nimrod had come to life again in Tammuz. Among the Druids-Celts, the oak tree was sacred; among the Egyptians it was the palm tree; and in Rome, it was the fir tree, which was decorated with red berries during the Saturnalia."

Walsh, *Curiosities of Popular Customs*, Page 242

Fredrick J. Haskins, who wrote a book called, *Answers to Questions*, states "the Christmas tree is from Egypt, and its origins date from a period long anterior to the Christian era." Did you know that the Christmas tree long preceded Christianity?

The prophet Jeremiah condemned as pagan the ancient Middle Eastern practice of cutting down trees, bringing them into homes, and decorating them. Of course, these were not really Christmas trees, because Jesus was not born until centuries later, and the use of Christmas trees was not introduced for many centuries after his birth. Apparently, in Jeremiah's time, the "heathen" would cut down trees, carve or decorate them in the form of a god or goddess, and overlay it with precious metals.

In Europe, pagans in the past cut down whole evergreen trees, brought them into their homes, and decorated them. That would have been far too destructive of nature, but during the Roman celebration of the feast of the Saturnalia, pagans did decorate their homes with clippings of evergreen shrubs. They also decorated living trees with bits of metal and replicas of their god, Bacchus.

Tertullian (circa 160-230), an early Christian leader and prolific writer, complained that too many fellow Christians had copied the pagan practice of adorning and decorating their homes, and this observance was adopted and painted with a Christian veneer by the church. Just as early Christians recruited Roman pagans by associating Christmas with the Saturnalia. Worshipers of the Asheira cult and its offshoots were recruited by the church with sanctioning "Christmas trees."

"Many Americans celebrate Christmas and X-mas. Others celebrate one or the other. And some of us celebrate holidays that, although unconnected with the (winter) solstice, occur near it: Hanukkah, Kamadan, and Kwanza."

John Silber's statement was correct when he wrote it in the year 2000. However, Islam follows a lunar calendar. Its holy days move earlier each year by about 11 days. Thus by 2010, the first day of Ramadan has moved back to August. Some people have traced the Christmas tree back at least as far as the prophet Jeremiah, who wrote the Book of Jeremiah in the Hebrew Scriptures (Old Testament).

Opposition to the Christmas tree was intense in past centuries. The early Christian church in the 3rd century C.E., strictly prohibited the decoration of their homes with evergreen boughs. The decorated Christmas tree only caught on in the mid-19th century.

Modern-day opposition continues: some condemn the Christmas tree because they believe that custom of cutting down a tree, erecting it in the home, and decorating it is a pagan custom for many people today. It is primarily as a secular symbol of hope for the New Year and the future, of the return of warmth to the earth. Its future is assured in spite of opposition.

The Source of Holly Wreaths, Yule Logs, and Mistletoe

The *Encyclopedia Americana* states, "the holly, the mistletoe, the yule log...are relics of pre-Christian times." In other words, they are paganism! The yule log was commonly used in a rite of Teutonic nature worship. Fredrick Haskin further states, "the use of Christmas wreaths is believed by authorities to be traceable to the pagan customs of decorating buildings and places of worship at the feast which took place at the same time as Christmas."

The *Encyclopedia Britannia* under "Celestials" exposes the origin of the holly wreath:

> European pagans brought holly sprays into their homes, offering them to the fiery people of the forest as a refuge from the harsh winter weather. During the Saturnalia, the Roman winter festival, branches of holly were exchanged as tokens of friendship. The earliest Roman Christians apparently used holly as a decoration at the Christmas season.

There are dozens of types of holly. My mother has planted scores of them. Virtually all of them come in male and female varieties, such as China Boy and China Girl, Blue Boy and Blue Girl, Blue Prince and Blue Princess. Female holly plants cannot have berries unless a nearby male plant pollinates them. However, these berries are not edible. It is easy to see why the holly wreath found its way into pagan rituals as a token of friendship and fertility.

The Roots of Mistletoe

Norse mythology recounts how the god Balder was killed from a mistletoe arrowshot by his rival god, Hoder, while fighting for the female, Nanna. Druid rituals use mistletoes to poison their human sacrificial victim. The Christian custom of "kissing under the mistletoe" is a later synthesis of the sexual license of Saturnalia with the druidic sacrificial cult. The *Encyclopedia Britannica* under "Santa Tales," states:

> "The European mistletoe is thought to have had special ritual significance in druidical ceremonies and lives of folklore today. Its special status as the Christmas mistletoe comes from Anglo-Saxon times."

Mistletoe is a parasite that lives on oak trees. Recall that the druids used to give mistletoes as herbal remedies to barren animals to make them fertile. In mammals and humans, it is from the egg (or ovum, as it is properly called, where reproduction begins). The herb was called "all healer" in Celtic. Like the mistletoe, holly berries were also thought to be sacred to the sun god. The original "sun log" came to be called the "yule log." Yule simply means "wheel," which has been a pagan representation of the sun during the Christmas season. You may hear many people commonly speak of the "sacred yuletide season." How awesome, interesting, and sobering are the facts of history!

When Was Jesus Born?

Jesus was born in the fall of the year. Popular myth plots his birth on Dec. 25th in the year 1 C.E. The New Testament gives no date or year for the birth of Jesus. The pagan mid-winter festival is the alleged birthdate of Jesus of Nazareth, and with a few other pagan goodies thrown in to make their takeover more palatable. December 25th was not selected because it was the birth of Christ or because it was even near it, but because it coincided with the idolatrous pagan festival, Saturnalia—and this celebration must be carefully examined.

In any event, we do not know the exact date of Jesus's birth. While God certainly could have made it known, he chose to keep it from the world!

Joseph A. Fitzmyer, professor of Emeritus of Biblical Studies at the Catholic University of America, member of the Pontifical Biblical commission, and former president of the Catholic Biblical Association, writing in the Catholic Church's official commentary on the New Testament, writes about the dates of Jesus' birth. "Though the year of

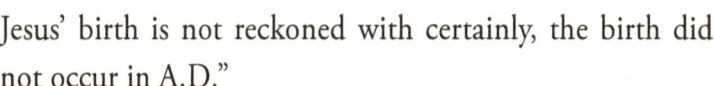

Jesus' birth is not reckoned with certainly, the birth did not occur in A.D."

The Christian era, which is supposed to have its starting point in the year of Jesus' birth, is based on a miscalculation introduced in Ca. 533 by Dionysius Exiguus. The *Depascha Computus*, an anonymous document believed to have been written in North Africa around 243 C.E., placed Jesus' birth on March 28th. Clement, a bishop of Alexandria (D. Ca. 215 C.E.) thought Jesus was born on November 18th. Based on historical records, Fitzmyer guesses that Jesus' birth occurred on September 11th, B.C.E.

The earliest gospel, St. Mark's, written about 65 C.E., begins with the baptism of an adult Jesus. This suggests that the earliest Christians lacked interest in knowledge of Jesus's birthdate. The year of Jesus' birth was determined by Dionysius Exiguus, a Scythian monk, Abbott of a Roman monastery. His calculation went as follows: in the Roman pre-Christian era, years were counted from Ab URBE Condita, "the founding of the city of Rome." Thus 1 AUC signifies the year Rome was founded, 5 AUC signifies the fifth year of Rome's reign, etc. ...

Dionysius received a tradition that the Roman emperor Augustus reigned 43 years and was followed by the emperor Tiberius. According to Luke 3:1, 23, when Jesus turned 30 years old, it was the 15th year of Tiberius' reign. If Jesus was 30 years old in Tiberius' reign, then he lived 15 years under Augustus, (placing Jesus' birth in Augustus' 28th year of reign). Augustus took power in 727 AUC, therefore, Dionysius put Jesus' birth in 754 AUC.

However, according to Luke 1:5, we learn about John's (AKA John the Baptist by many professing Christians today) birth announced to Zacharias. (V5) *There was in the days of Herod, the King of Judea, a certain priest named Zacharias, of the division of Abijah. His wife was of the daughters of Aaron, and her name was Elizabeth.*

Mathews 2:1: *Now after Jesus was born in Bethlehem of Judea in the days of Herod the king, behold, wise men from the east came to Jerusalem.* In this chapter, it takes place after birth in the days of Herod. (V9) *When they heard the king, "they" departed; and behold, the star which "they" had seen in the east went before "them," until it came and stood over where the young child was.* (At this time, Jesus was no longer an infant, but a young child, perhaps 2 years old). (V10) *When "they" had seen the star, "they" rejoiced with exceedingly great joy.*

(V11) *And when "they" had come into the house (not stable, nor cave, but in the house), they saw the young child with Mary his mother, and fell down and worshiped him. And when "they" had opened "their" treasures, "they" presented gifts to him … (Jesus): gold, frankincense, and myrrh.* They were mentioned nine times, and then were mentioned one time. Their one time was when he was a young child. But in the Bible, it never tells us the exact amount of wise men there were. But for some reason, I have heard—even out of the mouths of ministers—claims that there were only three wise men that showed up.

According to the history when they went to present themselves to the king, they never traveled alone, but with their servants and packs loaded with their own supplies ... taking food and water, and riding on camels. When Mary, Joseph, and baby Jesus took flight into Egypt, it wasn't like today:

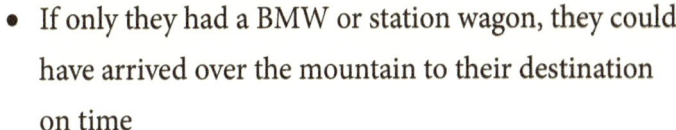

- They had no cell phones
- They did not have amenities today such as home phones or the internet
- They had to go over passages full of changes and danger
- Perhaps they bought a tent to shield them from inclement weather, for there were no hotels
- If only they had a BMW or station wagon, they could have arrived over the mountain to their destination on time

They had to escape the king. He sent forth a decree to put to death all the male children ... two years and under.

What Does God Say about Christians Who Practice Pagan Customs?

First, let's look at what happened to the ones who did in the biblical days starting in Lev. 18:21, 29: *(V21) And you should not let any of your descendants pass through the fire of Molech, nor shall you profane the name of your god: I am the lord.* (V29) *For whoever commits any of these abominations, the person who commits them shall be cut off from among their people.*

In ancient times, anyone who practiced false pagan customs with the worship of the true God was put to death. Let's look at 2 Kings 17:33: *They feared the lord, and served their own gods, after the manner of the nations whom they carried away from there.* Did you grasp this? Yes, they feared the true God while serving other gods.

CHAPTER 2

New Year's

History

In 45 B.C., New Year's Day is celebrated on January 1st for the first time in history, as the Julian calendar takes effect. Soon after becoming Roman Dictator, Julius Caesar decided that the traditional Roman calendar was in dire need of reform. Introduced around the 7th century B.C., the Roman calendar attempted to follow the lunar cycle, but frequently fell out of phase with the seasons and had to be corrected. In addition, the pontifices, the Roman body charged with overseeing the calendar, often abused its authority by adding days to extend political terms or interfere with elections.

In designing his new calendar, Caesar enlisted the aid of Sosogenes, an Alexandrian astronomer, who advised him to do away with the lunar cycle entirely and follow the solar year, as did the Egyptians. The year was calculated to be 365 and ¼ days, and Caesar added 67 days to 45 B.C., making 46 B.C. begin on January 1st, rather than in March. He also decreed that every four years, a day be added to February, thus theoretically keeping his calendar from falling out of step. Shortly before his assassination in 44 B.C., he changed the name of the month Quintilis to Julius (July) after himself. Later, the month of Sextilis was renamed Augustus (August) after his successor.

Celebration of New Year's Day in January fell out of practice during the Middle Ages, and even those who strictly adhered to the Julian calendar did not observe the New Year exactly on January 1. The reason for the latter was that Caesar and Sosogenes failed to calculate the correct value for the solar year as 365.242199 days, not 365.25 days. Thus, an 11-minute-a-year error added seven days by the year 1000, and 10 days by the mid-15th century.

The Roman church became aware of this problem, and in the 1570s, Pope Gregory XIII commissioned Jesuit astronomer, Christopher Clavius, to come up with a new calendar. In 1582, the Gregorian calendar was implemented, omitting 10 days for that year and establishing the new rule that only one of every four centennial years should be a leap year. Since then, people around the world have gathered en masse on January 1st to celebrate the precise arrival of the New Year.

New Year's Eve by the Numbers

New Year's Eve is all about numbers. Indeed, we spend the entire day counting down the hours until 11p.m., when we start counting the minutes, which we do until 11:59 p.m., when we start counting the seconds. Suffice it to say, there isn't another day of the year when more people actually take the time to count.

Of course, the day itself is about the acquisition of a new number. This year, it's the transfer from 2015 to 2016. But there are so many other numbers at play over the New Year's holiday, from the amount of celebrants and spectators to the percentage of people who will make a resolution (and how many glasses of champagne they will drink before they honor it).

Here's a look at New Year's Eve (and New Year's Day) by the numbers:

1. 1 million: the amount of people expected to attend America's largest New Year's Eve celebration in New York City's Times Square. And 1 billion people from around the world will watch the famed ball drop on TV.

2. 3,200: How much it costs in dollars to get a direct view of the ball drop at the Marriott Marquis' "ultimate New Year's Eve Times Square party."

3. 1907: The first year a lighted ball was dropped over Times Square in honor of the New Year.

4. 2: The number of times the ball didn't drop in Times Square for New Year's (thanks to lighting restrictions during World War II).

5. 8: The number of years organizers modified the ball to look like a "big apple" during the 1980s before thinking better of the idea.

6. 11,875: How many pounds the current ball weighs. It's that heavy because it has 2,688 Waterford crystal triangles capable of producing billions of different light patterns.

7. 2,000: How many pounds of confetti organizers will drop on the crowd in Times Square.

8. 33.7: The average degrees Fahrenheit at 12 a.m. on January 1st in New York City.

9. 44: The percent of American adults that say they will kiss someone at the stroke of midnight.

10. 45: The percent of American adults that say they will make a New Year's resolution. Of those, just 46 percent are expected to keep their resolution six months later.

11. 22: The percent of people that will be fast asleep before midnight.

12. 360 million: How many glasses of sparkling wine will be served during the holiday season.

13. 25: The percentage of all champagne bottles sold in the United States that will be purchased in the week between Christmas and New Year's Day. Each bottle will have about 49 million bubbles inside and should be held at 45-degree angle before popping.

14. 10,000: The number of costumed revelers that will march in Philadelphia's Mummers Parade, the United States' oldest folk festival, dating back to the mid-17th century.

15. 1890: The first time residents of Pasadena, California, held the New Year's Day Tournament of Roses Parade.

16. 18 million: The estimated number of flowers used in the 42 floats created for the parade, which 39 million Americans are expected to watch on TV.

Mark Johanson. "New Year's Eve by the Numbers." *International Business Times.* December 31, 2012.

CHAPTER 3

Leap Year

History

Nearly every four years, we add an extra day to the calendar in the form of February 29, also known as Leap Day. Put simply, these additional 24 hours are built into the calendar to ensure that it stays in line with the Earth's movement around the Sun.

While the modern calendar contains 365 days, the actual time it takes for Earth to orbit its star is slightly longer—roughly 365.2421 days. The difference might seem negligible, but over decades and centuries that missing quarter of a day per year add up. To ensure consistency with the true astronomical year, it is necessary to add in an extra day periodically to make up the lost time and get the calendar back in synch with the heavens.

The Egyptians were among the first to calculate the need for a leap year, but the practice didn't arrive in Europe until the reign of the Roman dictator, Julius Caesar. Before then, the Roman calendar had operated on a muddled lunar model that regularly required adding an extra month to maintain celestial consistency.

Finally, in 46 B.C., Caesar and the astronomer Sosogenes revamped the Roman calendar to include 12 months and 365 days. This "Julian Calendar" also accounted for the slightly longer solar year by adding a leap day to every fourth years.

Caesar's model helped realign the Roman calendar, but it had one small problem. Since the solar year is only .242 days longer than the calendar year and not an even .25, adding a leap year every four years actually leaves an annual surplus of roughly 11 minutes.

This minute discrepancy meant that the Julian calendar drifted off course by 1 day every 128 years, and by the 14th century, it had strayed 10 days off the solar year. To fit the glitch, Pope Gregory XIII instituted a revised "Gregorian Calendar" in 1582.

In this model, leap year occur every four years except for years evenly divisible by 100 and not by 400. For example, the year 1900 was not a leap year because it was divisible by 100, but not 400. The Pope's updated calendar remains in use to this day, but it's still not perfect—experts note that the remaining discrepancies will need to be addressed in around 10,000 years

---

"Why Do We Have Leap Year?" WWW History Channel.

CHAPTER 4

April Fools' Day

All Fools' Day

On this day in 1700, English pranksters begin popularizing the annual traditions of April Fools' Day by playing practical jokes on each other. Although the day, also called All Fools' Day, has been celebrated for several centuries by different cultures, its exact origins remain a mystery.

Some historians speculate that April Fools' Day dates back to 1582, when France switched from the Julian calendar to the Gregorian calendar, as called for by the Council of Trent in 1563. People who were slow to get the news or failed to recognize that the start of the New Year had moved to January 1 and continued to celebrate it during the last week of March through April became the butt of jokes and hoaxes. These included having paper fish placed on their backs and being referred to as "poisson d'avril" (April fish), said to symbolize a young, easily caught fish or a gullible person.

Earlier Celebrations

Historians have also linked April Fools' Day to ancient festivals such as Hilaria, which was celebrated in Rome at the end of March and involved people dressing up in disguises. There's also speculation that April Fools' Day was tied to the Vernal equinox, or first day of spring in the northern hemisphere, when Mother Nature fooled people with changing, unpredictable weather.

April Fools' Day spread throughout Britain during the 18th century. In Scotland, the tradition became a two-day event, starting with "hunting the gowk," in which people were sent on phony errands (gowk is a word for cuckoo bird, a symbol for fool) and followed by Tatite Day, which involved pranks played on people's derrieres, such as pinning fake tails or "kick me" signs on them.

April Fools' Day Tricks

In modern times, people have gone to great lengths to create elaborate April Fools' Day hoaxes. Newspaper, radio and TV stations and websites have participated in the April tradition of reporting outrageous fictional claims that have fooled their audiences.

In 1957, the BBC reported that the Swiss farmers were experiencing a record spaghetti crop and showed footage of people harvesting noodles from trees; numerous viewers were fooled. In 1985, sports illustrated tricked many of its readers when it ran a made-up article about a rookie pitcher named Sidd Finch who could throw a fast ball over 168 miles per hour. In 1996, Taco Bell, the fast-food restaurant chain, duped people when it announced it had agreed to purchase Philadelphia's liberty bell. In 1998, after Burger King advertised a "left-handed whopper," scores of clueless customers requested the fake sandwich.

CHAPTER 5

St. Patrick's Day

Religious Feast Day

Every year on March 17, the Irish and the Irish-at-heart across the globe observe St. Patrick's Day. What began as a religious feast day for the patron saint of Ireland has become an international festival celebrating Irish culture with parades, dancing, special foods, and a whole lot of green.

Was St. Patrick Irish?

St. Patrick is known as the patron saint of Ireland. True, he was not born Irish. But he has become an integral part of the Irish heritage, mostly through his service across Ireland of the 5th century. Patrick was born in the latter half of the 4th century A.D. There are differing views about the exact year and place of his birth. According to one school of opinion, he was born about 390 A.D., while the other school says it is about 373 A.D.

Again, his birthplace is said to be in either Scotland or Roman England. His real name was probably Maewyn Suscat. Though Patricius was his Romanized name, he later came to be familiar as Patrick.

Patrick was the son of Calpurnius, a Roman-British army officer. He was growing up as nationally as other kids in Britain. However, one day a band of pirates landed in south Wales and kidnapped this boy along with many others. Then they sold him into slavery in Ireland. He was there for six years, mostly imprisoned.

This was when changes came to him. He dreamed of having seen God. Legend says God told him to escape in a getaway ship. Finally, he did escape and went to Britain and then to France. There he joined a monastery, and studied under St. Germain, the bishop of Auxerre. He spent around 12 years in training. And when he became a bishop, he dreamed that the Irish where calling him back to Ireland to tell them about God.

The Confessio, Patrick's spiritual autobiography, is the most important document regarding this. It tells of a dream after his return to Britain, in which one, Victoricus, delivered him a letter headed, "The Voice of the Irish," so he set out for Ireland with the pope's blessing. There he converted the Gaelic Irish, who were then mostly pagans, to Christianity.

He was confident in the Lord, so he journeyed far and wide, baptizing and confirming with untiring zeal. And, in a diplomatic fashion, he brought gifts to a kinglet here and a lawgiver there, but accepted none from any. Indeed, Patrick was quite successful at winning converts through active preaching. He made important converts even among the royal families. This fact upset the Celtic Druids, so they arrested Patrick several times, but he escaped each time.

For 20 years, he traveled throughout Ireland, establishing monasteries across the country. He also set up schools and churches that would aid him in conversion. He developed a native clergy, fostered the growth of monasticism, established dioceses, and held church councils.

Patrick's doctrine is considered orthodox and has been interpreted as anti-Pelagian. Although he is not particularly noted as a man of learning, a few of his writings remain extant: his confession, a reply to his detractors, and several letters.

The Lorica ("breastplate"), a famous hymn attributed to Patrick, may date to a later period. By the end of the 7th century, Patrick had become a legendary figure, and the legends have continued to grow since then. It is said that he used the three-leafed shamrock to explain the concept of what many Christians believe in to be known as the trinity and to which many Christians today refer as the combination of the Father, Son, and Holy Spirit. Hence, its strong association with his day and name.

Legend also has that Saint Patrick had put the curse of God on venomous snakes in Ireland and drove all the snakes into the sea where they drowned. True, these are mostly legends, but after some 1500 years, these legends have been inseparably combined with the facts. Together they have helped us know much about the saint and the spirit behind the celebration of that day.

Patrick's mission in Ireland lasted for over 20 years. He died on March 17, 461 A.D. That day has been commemorated as St. Patrick's Day ever since.

(http://www.theholidayspot.com/patrick/historyofpatrick.htm)

Leprechauns

In Irish mythology, a leprechaun is a type of male faeria, said to inhabit the island of Ireland, before the Celts arrived. Leprechauns usually take the form of old men who enjoy partaking in mischief. The originally Irish name for these figures of folklore is lobarcin, meaning small-bodied fellow. Their trade is that of a cobbler or shoemaker. They are said to be very rich, having many treasure crocks buried during wartime. According to legend, if anyone keeps an eye fixed upon one, he cannot escape, but the moment the gaze is withdrawn, he vanishes.

Leprechauns rarely appear in what would be classed as a folktale. Stories about leprechauns are generally very brief and generally have local names attached to them.

In most tales and stories, leprechauns are depicted as

generally harmless creatures, who enjoy solitude and live in remote locations, while in others they are depicted as ill-natured and mischievous, with a mind for cunning. The leprechauns of legend are believed to have hidden their gold at the end of each of the rainbows that glow in the beautiful sky after a storm in the clouds above.

(http://www.hellokids.com/c_15081/reading-and-learning/
    stories-for-children/st-patrick-s-day-history-and-fun-facts/
    leprechauns)

When I was a girl, I was in a 4-H Club, in Henryville, Indiana. After the first meeting or two, us young girls still had not came up with a name for our club. So our leader had called the Catholic priest from St. Francis Xavier Parrish to come to one of the meetings. He told us the story of St. Patrick and many of the legends of Ireland, including the shamrock. At the end, us girls all put a name of what we wanted to be called on a piece of paper and put it in a plate, where cookies once were. That's how we became the Henryville Shamrocks.

The name, shamrock, comes from the Irish for seamrog, which is the diminutive of the Irish word for clover (seamair) and means simply "little clover" or "young clover."

(Wikipedia free encyclopedia)

On St. Patrick's Day, Why Do People Wear Green?

Green on St. Patrick's Day is a tradition that started in the 17th century, when green ribbons and shamrocks were worn to celebrate Ireland's patron saint. The tradition was popularized by Irish immigrants in the United States, who believed that wearing green made you invisible to leprechauns, fairy creatures who would pinch anyone they could see. Pinching those who didn't wear green was meant to remind them that leprechauns could sneak up at any given time. Still, only around half of Americans chose to deck themselves out in green for the holiday.

(http://www.bhg.com/holidays/st-patricks-day/traditions/
how-to-wear-green-for-st-patricks-day/#page=0)

CHAPTER 6

Easter

Is Easter Biblical?

Since it does arrive once a year and many preach that it is the day that supposedly Jesus had risen on that day, then it's got to be biblical, right?

However, Easter has nothing to do with God and is condemned in Scripture in the strongest possible terms. The apostate false church simply adopted it into practice, and enforced it on all citizens in the empire through the vehicle of the civil government.

Although many celebrate it, including thousands of ministers, this encourages their churches to partake and celebrate this pagan heathen festival that God himself is totally against. This celebration includes trick shows, egg hunts, baskets of candy, parades, coloring eggs, and even tricking little children's minds into believing that rabbits lay chicken eggs—how foolish! Then they have sunrise services for their members that once again God himself is totally against. Easter requires close attention and this chapter examines it very carefully

Does the Word of God mention Easter? Let's pay close attention to Acts 12:1. King Herod began to persecute the church, culminating in the brutal death of the apostle James by the sword. This pleased the Jews so much that Herod also took the apostle Peter prisoner. The plan was to deliver him to the Jews later.

Verse 3 says, "Then were the days of unleavened bread." The new testament church was observing these feast days described in Leviticus 23. Now let's read verse 4: and when he {King Herod} had apprehended him, he put him in prison, and delivered him to four squads {16} soldiers to keep him, intending to bring him before the people after Passover. This passage is "not" talking about Easter. How do we know?

The word translated as Easter is the Greek word, pascha {derived from the Hebrew word pesach—there is no original Greek word for Passover}, and it has only one meaning—it always means Passover. It can never mean Easter for this reason—we never find a Hebrew word used in the Greek New Testament. Once again, my readers, this Hebrew word can "only" refer to Passover. And, other translations, including the Revised Standard Version, correctly render this word, Passover.

Instead of endorsing Easter, this verse really proves that the church was still observing the supposedly Jewish Passover ten years "after" the death of Jesus. Nowhere in the Scriptures will we find that God authorized Easter nor Lent, rabbits, and chickens having intercourse with rabbits to have Easter bunnies, egg hunts, baskets of candy, parades, trick shows, coloring eggs, etc., although it does mention hot cross buns and sunrise services as abominations, which once again God himself strongly condemns.

CHAPTER 7

Mother's Day

U.S. History

Mother's day is a modern celebration honoring one's own mother, as well as motherhood, maternal bonds, and the influence of mothers in society. It is celebrated on various days in many parts of the world, most commonly in the months of March or May. It complements similar celebrations honoring family members such as Father's Day and Sibling's Day.

The celebration of Mother's Day began in the United States in the early twentieth century, but is not related to the many celebrations of mothers and motherhood that have occurred throughout the world over thousands of years. For example, it does not include the Greek cult of Cybele, the roman festival of Hilaria, or the Christian mothering Sunday celebration or generally, a celebration of the mother church—not motherhood. Despite this, in some countries, Mother's Day has become synonymous with these older traditions.

Founding

The modern American holiday of Mother's Day was first celebrated in 1908, when Anna Jarvis held a memorial for her mother at Saint Andrew's Methodist Church in Grafton, West Virginia. It now holds the International Mother's Day shire.

Her campaign to make mother's day a recognized holiday in the United States began in 1905, the year her beloved mother, Ann Reeves Jarvis, died. Anna's mission was to honor her own mother by continuing work she started and to set aside a day to honor mothers, "the person who has done more for you than anyone in the world."

Anna's mother, Ann Jarvis, was a peace activist who cared for wounded soldiers on both sides of the Civil War and created Mother's Day work clubs to address public health issues. In 1908, the United States congress rejected a proposal to make an official holiday, among jokes that they would have to proclaim also a "mother-in-law's day.

Due to the campaign efforts of Anna Varvis, by 1911 all states in the U.S. observed the holiday, with some of them officially recognizing Mother's Day as a local holiday, the first in 1910 being West Virginia, Jarvis' home state.

In 1914, Woodrow Wilson signed the proclamation creating Mother's Day, the second Sunday in May, as a national holiday to honor mothers. Although Jarvis was successful in founding Mother's Day, she soon became resentful of the commercialization and was angry that companies would profit from the holiday. By the early 1920s, Hallmark and other companies started selling Mother's Day cards.

Jarvis became so embittered by what she saw as misinterpretation and exploitation that she protested and even tried to rescind Mother's Day. The holiday that she had worked so hard for was supposed to be about sentiment—not about profit. Jarvis' intention for the holiday had been for people to appreciate and honor mothers by writing a personal letter, by hand, expressing love and gratitude, rather than buying gifts and pre-made cards.

Jarvis organized boycotts and threatened lawsuits to try to stop the commercialization. She crashed a candy maker's convention in Philadelphia in 1923. Two years later she protested at a confab of the American War Mothers, which raised money by selling carnations, the flower associated with Mother's Day, and was arrested for disturbing the peace. Jarvis' holiday was adopted by other countries and it is now celebrated all over the world.

Mothering Sunday

The history of Mother's Day is centuries old and the earliest Mother's Day celebrations can be traced back to the spring celebrations of ancient Greece. Christians in England celebrated a day to honor Mary, the mother of Christ. The holiday was later expanded in its scope to include all mothers, and named as the Mothering Sunday, celebrated on the fourth Sunday of Lent.

Mothering Sunday honored the mothers of England. During this time, many of the England's poor worked as servants for the wealthy. As most jobs were located far from their homes, the servants would live at the houses of their employers. On Mothering Sunday, the servants would have the day off and were encouraged to return home and spend the day with their mothers. A special cake, called the mothering cake, was often brought along to provide a festival touch.

As Christianity spread throughout Europe, the celebration changed to honor the "mother church," the spiritual power that gave them life and protected them from harm. Over time, the church festival blended with the Mothering Sunday celebration. People began honoring their mothers, as well as the church. With the passage of time, the practice of this fantastic tradition ceased slowly.

The English colonists settled in America discontinued the tradition of Mothering Sunday because of lack of time. In the United States, Mother's Day was loosely inspired by the British day and was first suggested after the American Civil War by social activist, Julia Ward Howe. Howe (who wrote the words to the *Battle Hymn of the Republic*) was horrified by the carnage of the Civil War and the Franco Prussian War and so, in 1870, she too issued a manifesto for peace at international peace conferences in London and Paris (it was much like the later Mother's Day peace proclamation).

During the Franco Prussian War in the 1875, Julia began a one-woman peace crusade and made an impassioned appeal to womanhood to rise against war. She composed in Boston a powerful plea that same year (generally considered to be the original Mother's Day Proclamation) translated into several languages and distributed widely.

In 1872, she went to London to promote an international woman's peace congress. She began promoting the idea of a Mother's Day for peace to be celebrated on June 2, honoring peace, motherhood and womanhood. In Boston, she initiated a mother's peace day observance on the second Sunday in June, a practice that was to be established as an annual event and practiced for at least 10 years. The day was, however, mainly intended as a call to unite women against war.

It was due to her efforts that in 1873, women in 18 cities in America held a Mother's Day for Peace gathering. Howe rigorously championed the cause of official holiday on the day. She held meetings every year at Boston on Mother's Peace Day and took care that the day was well observed.

The celebrations died out when she turned her efforts to working for peace and women's right in other ways. Howe failed in her attempt to get the formal recognition of a Mother's Day for Peace. Her remarkable contribution in the establishment of Mother's Day, however, remains in the fact that she organized a Mother's Day dedicated to peace.

It is a landmark in the history of Mother's Day in the sense that this was to be the precursor to the modern Mother's Day celebrations. To acknowledge Howe's achievements, a stamp was issued in her honor in 1988.

It should be well to remember that Howe's idea was influenced by Ann Marie Reeves Jarvis, a young Appalachian homemaker who starting in 1858, had attempted to improve sanitation through what she called "mother's friendship day." in the 1900s. At a time when most women devoted their time solely to their family and homes, Jarvis was working to assist in the healing of the nation after the Civil War. She organized women throughout the Civil War to work for better sanitary conditions for both sides and in 1868, she began work to reconcile union and confederate neighbors. Ann was instrumental in saving thousands of lives by teaching women in her mother's friendship clubs the basics of nursing and sanitation, which she had learned from her famous physician brother, James Reeves, M.D.

In part of the United States, it was customary to plant tomatoes outdoors after Mother's Work Days (and not before). It was Jarvis, who finally succeeded introducing Mother's Day in the sense as we celebrate it today.

Anna graduated from the female seminary in Wheeling and taught in Grafton for a while. Later she moved to Philadelphia with her family. Anna had spent many years looking after her ailing mother. This is why she preferred to remain a spinster. When her mother died in Philadelphia on May 9, 1905, Anna missed her greatly. So did her sister,

Elsinore, whom she looked after as well.

Anna felt children often neglected to appreciate their mother enough while the mother was still alive. Now, she intended to start a Mother's Day, as an honoring of the mothers. In 1907, two years after her mother's death, Anna Jarvis disclosed her intention to her friends who supported her cause wholeheartedly.

So supported by her friends, Anna decided to dedicate her life to her mother's cause and to establish Mother's Day to honor mothers, living and dead. She started the campaign to urge ministers, businessmen, and congressman in declaring a national Mother's Day holiday. She hoped this holiday would increase respect for parents and strengthen family bonds.

Early History of Mother's Day

The earliest history of Mother's Day dates back to the ancient annual spring festival the Greeks dedicated to maternal goddesses.  The Greeks used the occasion to honor Rhea, wife of Cronus and the mother of many deities of Greek mythology.

Ancient Romans, too, celebrated a spring festival, called Hilaria dedicated to Cybele, a mother goddess. It is noted that ceremonies in honor of Cybele began some 250 years before Jesus was born. The celebration made on the Ides of March by making offerings in the temple of Cybele lasted three days and included parades, games, and masquerades. The celebrations were so scandalous, disgraceful, shocking, outrageous, sinful, wicked, criminal, appalling, inexcusable, intolerable, etc., that followers of Cybele were banished from Rome.

The Goddess, Rhea, Wife of Cronus

Rhea is Greek for pea (pronounced re-aal) is the Titaness daughter of the earth goddess, Gaia, and the sky god, Uranus, in Greek mythology and sister and wife to Cronus. In early traditions, she is known as "the mother of gods" and, therefore, is strongly associated with Gaia and Cybele, who have similar functions.

The classical Greeks saw her as the mother of the Olympian goddesses and gods, but not as an Olympian goddess in her own right. The Romans identified her with Magna Mater (their form of Cybele), and the goddess, Ops. Rhea had no strong local cult of identifiable activity under her control. She was originally worshipped in the island of Crete, where according to myth, she saved the new-born Zeus from being devoured (eaten) by Cronus, by substituting a stone for the infant god and entrusting him to the care of her attendants, the Curetes. These attendants afterward became the bodyguards of Zeus and the priests of Rhea. Their rhythmic, raucous chants and dances, accompanied by the tympanon (a wide, handheld drum) and the clashing of bronze shields and cymbals, provoked a state of religious ecstasy. This may have been the source for the use of a tympanon in Cybele's rites. In historical times, the resemblances between the two goddesses were so marked that some Greeks regarded Cybele as their own Rhea, who had deserted her original home on Mount Ida in Crete and fled to the wilds of Phrygia to escape Cronus.

Virgil expressed the reverse view, and it is probably true that cultural contacts with the mainland formed into Rhea or identified with an existing local goddess and her rites. In *Homer*, Rhea is the mother of the gods, although not a universal mother like Cybele, the Phrygian great mother, with whom she was later identified. In the *Argonautica* by Apollonius of Rhodes, the fusion of Rhea and Phrygian Cybele is complete. "Upon the Mothers depend the winds, the ocean, the whole earth beneath the snowy seat of Olympus; whenever she leaves the mountains and climbs to the great vault of heaven, Zeus himself, the son of Cronus, makes way, and all the other immortal gods likewise make way for the dread goddess," the seer Mopsus tells Jason in *Argonautica*. Jason climbed to the sanctuary high on Mount Dindymon to offer sacrifice and libations to placate the goddess, so that the Argonauts might continue on their way.

For her Temenos (temple), they wrought an image of the goddess, an Xoanon, from a vine-stump. There "they called upon the mother of Dindymon, mistress of all, the dweller in Phrygia, and with her Titias and Kyllenos, who alone of the many Cretan Dakryls of Ida are called 'guiders of destiny' and those who sit beside the Idaean Mother." They leapt and danced in their armour: "For this reason, the Phrygians still worship Rhea with tambourines and drums." (*Pea*, written by Henry George Liddell)

Rhea was one of the Titans, daughter of Uranus and Gaea. She was the sister and wife of Cronus, also a Titan. She was responsible for the way things flow in the kingdom of Cronus (her name means "that which flows"). Rhea and Cronus had six children: Hestia, Hades, Demeter, Poseidon, Hera and Zeus.

Cronus, afraid that he would be overthrown by his children, just like he had done with his father, so he decided to swallow all of them. However, he was tricked by Rhea, who managed to save Zeus from his father. When Zeus grew up, he forced his father to disgorge his siblings and eventually overthrew him.

Although Rhea was considered the "mother of gods," similarly to Gaea and Cybele, she did not have a strong cult or many followers. In art, she started appearing in the fourth century BC. Rhea was often symbolized as a pair of lions that pulled a celestial chariot. This symbol was often placed on city gates, the best-known example being that at the city of Mycenae, where two stone lions guarded the gates. Rhea is also called Ops or Rea.

(Robert Scott, "A Greek-English Lexicon." Perseus Digital Library, *Greek Mythology*)

CHAPTER 8

Father's Day

History

The campaign to celebrate the nation's fathers did not meet with the same excitement as celebrating Mother's Day—perhaps because, as one florist explained, "fathers haven't the same sentimental appeal that mothers have."

On July 5, 1908, a West Virginia church sponsored the nation's first event demonstrated to honor our fathers, a Sunday sermon in memory of the 362 men who had died in the previous December's explosions at the Fairmont Coal Company mines in Monongah. However, it was a one-time commemoration and not an annual holiday.

The next year, a Spokane, Washington woman name Sonora Smart Dodd, one of six children raised by a widower, tried to establish the official equivalent to Mother's Day for male parents. She went to the local churches, the YMCA, shopkeepers, and government officials to drum up support for her idea, and she was successful: Washington State celebrated the nation's first statewide Father's Day on July 19, 1910.

Slowly, the holiday spread. In 1916, President Wilson honored the day by using telegraphs signals to unfurl a flag in Spokane when he pressed a button in Washington, DC. In 1924, President Calvin Coolidge urged state governments to observe Father's Day. However, many men continued to distain the day. As one historian writes, "They scoffed at the holiday's sentimental attempts to domesticate manliness with flowers and gift-giving, or they derided the proliferation of such holidays as a commercial gimmick to sell more products—often paid for by the father himself."

My grandparents told me many years ago about the Great Depression and soon after, the stock market crash of October 1929, which sent Wall Street into a panic and wiped out millions of investors. This meant over the next several years, consumer spending and investment dropped, causing steep declines in industrial output and rising levels of unemployment as failing companies laid off many of their workers.

By 1933, when the Great Depression reached its peak, some 13 to 15 million Americans were unemployed and nearly half of the country's banks had failed. President Franklin Roosevelt helped lessen the worst effects of the Great Depression in the 1930s with rational stamps, also known as food stamps. However, the economy would not turn around until after 1939, when WW2 kicked American industry into high gear.

My grandparents had also told me of those who were blessed enough to remain employed, their wages fell and buying power decreased. Many Americans who were forced to buy on credit fell into debt, and number of fore-closures and repossessions climbed steadily. If you had a yard, you could grow a vegetable garden out of necessity. If you had some chickens you could sell some eggs, and a hen for someone's dinner. You could go to the movies on Saturdays, and buy yourself a bag of popcorn, and a drink for a whole nickel. If you had some cinnamon and could buy yourself a bag of sugar and flour and a package of yeast for 10 cents, you could make yourself some sweet bread. A package of bologna went a long ways. Even bubble gum you dare not throw away that same day, for there were only three pieces that came in the package, and you didn't know when you could afford to buy anymore.

Poor people were the ones who designed "salad." I grew up eating a lot of what my grandparents passed on to my parents. Here is a list of what some our relatives may have devoured during the Great Depression time. But remem-ber—never say what you will not eat or do to survive. They were our warriors, and showed us a path: cucumber sand-wiches, bacon sandwiches, gopher, deer, turtle, squirrels, rabbit, bear, roadkill, chicken feet and skin, pig guts, pig feet, pig tails, pig ears, pig nose, hamburger mixed with oatmeal (later came to be known as meatloaf), alligator tail, fish, dandelions, collar, mustard, turnip greens, pea-nut butter and jelly sandwiches, ketchup sandwiches, po-tato soup—water base—not milk, gravy and bread main dish, cornbread in milk, lard sandwiches, hot milk and rice, mayo sandwiches, toast with mashed potatoes and gravy, corn mush with milk, sweet potatoes, black-eyed susans, oatmeal meal with lard, tomato gravy and biscuits, onion sandwiches, sugar sandwiches, cookies were made with lard instead of with butter, turkey, wild-game, spaghetti with beans, and tomato sauce.

The American cheese sandwich was invented, because it was cheap to make, and didn't require refrigeration that many people who lived during this era didn't have. Butter and sugar sandwiches, bean soup, vegetable soup, eggs and grits, baked apples and peaches, wild berries, spam and mushroom soup, rag soup, garbanzo beans fried in chicken fat, salted, and eaten cold, popcorn, and bread, butter or peanut butter, and syrup or honey sandwiches. If you couldn't afford to buy it, perhaps you could grow it or you may need to find it to kill it.

Homeowners did their own repairs and found ingenious ways to make their homes functional and attractive. Many children were told stories by their mothers and grandparents, for many could not afford to buy a radio, or own a television, or even own one toy. Many people wore hand–me-downs. Many of the women learned how to sew, bake, and make homemade quilts. If you had a creative mind, you might be lucky to earn two cents by selling lemonade.

I have often heard those were the "good ole days." Were they? Sometimes, a store-brought gift just doesn't send the perfect message for Father's Day. Instead of buying him something, you could surprise him by making him something special. Your dad will love getting a unique gift that was made with love by you.

I was talking with my mother not too long ago (for some reason I've turned out a bit like her). I keep things even if some of them are at least 10 years old, like letters from my Uncle George. I remember when I was a young girl, one year I made a Father's Day card on a piece of construction paper. The crayon in my hand was very large, but I was trying to write him a message. On it, I printed, "Happy Fat," but then I had to start over, for there wasn't enough room, but the message ended as, "Happy Father Day, I love you."

I can still see Dad's expression on his face, as he sat with his favorite blue shirt on at the dinner table, looking at the cake. He is no longer with us, but memories last a very long time.

Happy Father's Day to all father's around the world.

Chapter 9

Thanksgiving Day

History

In 1621, the Plymouth colonists and Wampanoag Indians shared an autumn harvest feast that is acknowledged today as one of the first Thanksgiving celebrations in the colonies. For more than two centuries, days of thanksgiving were celebrated by individual colonies and states. It wasn't until 1863, in the midst of the Civil War, that President Abraham Lincoln proclaimed a national Thanksgiving Day to be held each November.

The First Thanksgiving

In September 1620, a small ship (c. 80-90 ft. on deck, 100-110 ft. overall) called the Mayflower transported the first English Separatists, known today as the Pilgrims, from Plymouth to the New World. There were 102 passengers, with a "crew estimated to have been about 30, but the exact number is unknown."

The Pilgrims were seeking a new home where they could freely practice their faith. Other individuals were lured by the promise of prosperity and land ownership in the New World. After a treacherous and uncomfortable ride across the open seas that most likely involved seasickness, death, and storms that lasted 66 days, they dropped anchor near the tip of Cape Cod, far north of their intended destination at the mouth of the Hudson River.

One month later, the Mayflower crossed Massachusetts Bay, where the Pilgrims, as they are now commonly known, began the work of establishing a village at Plymouth. Throughout that first brutal winter, they had no log cabins with fireplaces to help keep them warm from the bitter cold and to sleep in, so the colonists remained on board the ship.

Even though they may have stayed down below in the cabins, they were exposed to the cold, for they dared not build a fire upon the wooded ship—not even to keep their own body warm from the cruel bitter weather. If the Pilgrims had landed near a tropical island, it would have been far better for them. There would not have been any snow and they could have found fresh food to eat, such as roots, plants, wild cabbages, coconuts, greens, papayas, kiwis, oranges, lemons, strawberries, blueberries, oysters, and grapefruits to add to their diet and to give them what they lacked most—known to us as Vitamin C.

Because they lacked this important vitamin, the Pilgrims suffered from scurvy. This disease caused them to develop anemia, debility, exhaustion, edema (swelling) in some parts of their body, and loss of their teeth, which caused swollen bleeding gums and the opening of previously healed wounds. Scurvy particularly affected poorly nourished sailors until the end of the 18th century.

Without any source of Vitamin C, anyone who became pregnant was a danger to the unborn child, because the brain might not develop properly. The Pilgrims who did have scurvy showed symptoms of appetite loss, poor weight gain, diarrhea due to raw sewage on board the ship or nearby on the ground. They experienced rapid breathing, fever, irritability, tenderness, and discomfort in legs, swelling over long bones, bleeding in the stomach, and suffered from the feeling of paralysis and hemorrhage of the skin and mucous membranes, identified by a tiny pinpoint red mark. As if that wasn't enough pain, they would also develop bleeding in the eyes, plus corkscrew hair. You can view related pictures on JAMA Network-Dermatology.

On top of all that, the weather was unbearably cold, which could have caused heart attacks. What they saw when they looked out of the small portholes in the ship could have made them wonder if they could possibly endure the hardships. As they peered out toward the shoreline, they may have seen huge snow drifts piled higher than some of the trees. The wind most likely was cutting their skin, as the temperature was dropping, especially at nights. They had to cuddle close together for heat from each other to keep warm. The dead passengers may have been stored away from view of the others, until it stop snowing long enough to carry them outside.

Each year on the fourth Thursday in November,

Americans gather for a day of feasting with turkey, ham, wild game, cranberries, potatoes, greens, corn, mac-n-cheese, desserts, football, and family watching the Macy's parade. Thanksgiving celebrations would likely be unrecognizable to attendees of the original 1621 harvest meal. It continues to be a day for Americans to come together around the table.

Thanksgiving Dinner for the Pilgrims

Culinary historians believe that much of the Thanksgiving meal consisted of seafood, which is often absent from today's menus. Mussels in particular were abundant in New England and could be harvested easily, because they clung to rocks along the shoreline. The colonists occasionally served mussels with curds, a dairy product with a similar consistency to cottage cheese. Lobster, bass, clams and oysters might also have been part of the feast.

Squanto

Tisquantum ("Squanto") taught the pilgrims how to plant corn. He was born November 15, 1585, in Patuxet territory, Wampanoag Confederacy (now Plymouth Bay) and died on November 30, 1622. He was buried in Plymouth Hill, Massachusetts. He was a Catholic, converted from the Patuxet North American indigenous religion. During his lifetime, he crossed the Atlantic Ocean six times, traveling with colonists to London and back.

Etymology

Squanto (Tisquantum) is derived from a Wampanoag word for divine rage. This was likely a name he was given as an adult. *Smithsonian* magazine reports: "More than likely, Tisquantum was not the name he was given at birth. In that part of the Northeast, Tisquantum referred to rage, especially 'the world suffusing spiritual power' at the heart of coastal Indians' religious beliefs. When Tisquantum approached the Pilgrims and identified himself by that sobriquet, it was as if he had stuck out his hand and said, "Hello, I'm the wrath of God.""

CHAPTER 10

Halloween

Pagan vs. Christian Celebrations

Can you worship the true Jesus, and yet be pagan? A pagan who worships the one true God is rendering comfort to the enemy—Satan. Most people say it is their choice and they will do whatever they please. Many ministers see no conflict between Christianity and paganism. I know of a few organizations that won't celebrate them, just because that is what the Bible tells them to do. If there is one person among you who does not worship the same as you do, then do not do it. But then, I know of many church organizations that do not listen to what God says and yet calls themselves Christians. They don't want to be left out of the crowd. They want to be like the Jones church down the road. Everybody is doing it, so they have a "why not us?" attitude."

Can one truly be a Christian and serve pagan celebrations? If you are focused on what you believe, not what you do, you are thinking like a Christian. If you want to be a better pagan worshipper, stop worrying what others think of you, and continue to serve your God. Either you serve one master or continue serving the false savior of the world—Satan.

Celebrating Halloween

Recently, someone approached me asking me if any verse in the Bible states it is wrong to celebrate Halloween. If you are looking for verses that say, "Thou shalt not celebrate Halloween," it is not going to be in there. However, read Deut. 22:9-31. Notice that Israel was warned to not borrow the ways the pagan nations use to worship a false god and apply them to worship of the one true God. God is telling ancient Israel, and us by extension, that sinful pagan celebrations are not made right by applying them to God.

Let us suppose that after a woman marries a man, she talks sweet words about how other men before him treated her, and she keeps old love letters around the house for her husband to see, and places her X-rated pictures in her husband's view. How would the husband feel about those reminders of her former loves? Would he be convinced her devotion to him was full-hearted? Would such an explanation as, "When I read his love letters, and hold his pictures near my heart, I think of you instead," be very convincing?

One of the best examples in the Bible of what God thinks about humans borrowing and adapting false pagan celebrations and festivals (for holidays like Halloween and Christmas) for use toward worshipping him is found in

Ex. 32. This example occurs after God uses Moses and Aaron to free the children of Israel from Egyptian slavery. God calls Moses up the mount to receive instruction and the Ten Commandments engraved in stone.

The children of Israel must wait at the foot of the mountain for him to return. As time passes without his appearance, the Israelites grow restless. When Aaron, the high priest, sees this, he tells the people to bring him their jewelry, so that he can melt it down and make them an idol (shaped like a calf). The people responded immediately when this was done, as did God when he saw it!

... and they (the people) said, "These are your gods, O Israel, who brought you up out of the land of Egypt!" When Aaron saw this, he built an altar before it; and Aaron made proclamation and said, "Tomorrow shall be a festival to the Lord."

The Lord said to Moses, «Go down at once! Your people, whom you brought up out of the land of Egypt, have acted perversely ... Now let *me alone, so that my wrath may burn hot against them and I may consume them.* (Ex. 32:4, 5, 7, 10 NRSV)

Notice that God did not accept the worship of the golden calf as worship directed to him, despite Aaron proclaiming a festival to Him (vs.5) would occur the very next day. God's anger was kindled toward the Israelites for introducing pagan practices into their worship of him.

God was ready to destroy the Israelites, his chosen people with fire, the people he just recently freed from bondage out from Egypt, for such obedience until Moses intervened (Ex. 32:11-14).

Traditions used to worship false gods that are transferred to the one true God are unacceptable since the Bible says God never compromises with paganism. This is Paul making a point in 1 Cor. 10:19-22. What the pagans practiced did not honor the one true God, regardless of how much sincerity or faith they had. The same goes for the celebrations used in holidays like Halloween, Leap Year, St. Patrick's Day, and New Year's Day.

CHAPTER 11

Yom Kipper

History

Did you know? Hall of Famer Sandy Koufax, one of the most famous Jewish Athletes in American sports, made national headlines when he refused to pitch in the first game of the 1965 World Series, because it fell on Yom Kippur. When Koufax's replacement Don Drysdale was pulled from the game for poor performance, he told the Los Angeles Dodgers' manager, Walter Alston, "I bet you wish I was Jewish, too."

Jewish texts recount that during biblical times, Yom Kippur was the only day on which the high priest could enter the inner sanctum of the Holy Temple in Jerusalem. There, he would perform a series of rituals and sprinkle blood from sacrificed animals on the Ark of the Covenant, which contained the Ten Commandments.

Through this complex ceremony, he made atonement and asked for God's forgiveness on behalf of all the people of Israel. The tradition is said to have continued until the destruction of the Second Temple by the Romans in 70

A.D. It was then adapted into a service for rabbis and their congregations in individual synagogues.

According to HistoryChannel.com, "Yom Kippur means 'Day of Atonement' and refers to the annual Jewish observance of fasting, prayers, and repentance." Yom Kippur fasting lasts for 25 hours and begins on the evening before Yom Kippur. It ends after nightfall on Yom Kippur.

(ChristianBroadcastingNetwork.Com\Bible Study\Yom Kippur)

CHAPTER 12

Famous Jewish People Who Wrote Holiday Songs

Celebrating the Holidays with Song

When I was a young girl, every Christmas holiday we used to get out the old Christmas records and sing along with my favorite songs. I never cared where they had come from or who had written them, I just thought it was because it was baby Jesus' birthday. Many of the holiday song writers back in the 60s were Jewish people.

Notice I said "holiday" songs and not "Christmas" songs. Irving Berlin turns Easter into a fashion show and Christmas into a holiday about snow. Like the songs of "Easter Parade," and, of course, "White Christmas." But it wasn't just Berlin. Here are the top 10 holiday songs written by Jewish people:

1. *White Christmas*
   Music and lyrics by Irving Berlin
   Bing Crosby's version is the best-selling single ever.

2. *The Christmas Song*

> Music and lyrics by Mel Torme and Bob Wells (more
> commonly known as Chestnuts Roasting on an Open
> Fire) Sung by Mel Torme and Judy Garland. These first
> two picks are traditional Christmas songs. They men-
> tion the holiday explicitly, are full of heartfelt sentiment,
> and may cause a few drops of tears.

3. *Let It Snow, Let It Snow, Let It Snow*

> Music by Julie Styne and lyrics by Sammy Cahn
> Sung by Frank Sinatra

4. *I've Got My Love to Keep Me Warm*

> Music and lyrics by Irving Berlin

5. *I'll Be Home For Christmas*

> Music by Buck Ram and lyrics by Walter Ken
> Sung by Johnny Mathis
> Like *White Christmas* and *Have Yourself a Merry Little
> Christmas*, this song was popular during WW2, and it
> appeals to a certain nostalgia and homesickness, not
> only on the parts of the troops abroad, but the loved
> ones at home.

6. *Sleigh Ride*

> Music by Leroy Anderson and lyrics by Mitchell Parrish
> Sung by Johnny Mathis

7. *Santa Baby*

> Music and lyrics by Joan Ellen Javits and Philip Springer
> Sung by Eartha Kitt in 1953
> This one is the closest thing to a jazz song in this list
> and a very enjoyable song. For some reason, Mrs. Claus
> wanted Santa to make all his rounds quickly, so he

could hurry down her chimney that night. So it's a love song and a seduction song, all in one. I am not sure how Santa was going to get a '54 convertible to fit into a chimney—then or today.

8. *Winter Wonderland*

> Music and lyrics by Felix Bernard
> Sung by Pat Boone
> The lyrics involve an impromptu wedding ceremony performed by a Parson Brown. The most interesting lyrical moment is the rhyme of "snow man" and "no, man."

9. *Silver Bells*

> Music by Jay Livingston and lyrics by Jay Livingston and Ray Evans.

> Sung by Bob Hope and Marilyn Maxwell in the motion picture *The Lemon Drop Kid.*

> This movie was filmed in July/August 1950 and released in March 1951. The first recorded version was by Bing Crosby and Carol Richards, released by Decca Records in October 1950. After the Crosby and Richards recording became popular, Hope and Maxwell were called back in late 1950 to refilm a more elaborate production of the song.

> *Silver Bells* started out as the questionable "tinkle bells." Said Ray Evans, "We never thought that tinkle had a double meaning until Jay went home and his first wife said, "Are you out of your mind? Do you know what the word tinkle mean? The word is slang for urination."

This song's inspiration has conflicting reports. Several periodicals and interviews cite the writer Jay Livingston stating that the song's inspiration came from the bells used by Santa Clauses and Salvation Army people on New York City street corners.

However, an interview with co-writer Ray Evans to NPR said that the song was inspired by a bell that sat on Ray and Jay's shared office desk. In the original version the lyrics were:

> Hear the snow crunch,
> See the kids bunch,
> This is Santa's big day.

but was later changed to

> Hear the snow crunch,
> See the kids bunch,
> This is Santa's big scene
> And above all this bustle you'll hear

> Silver bells, silver bells
> It's Christmas time in the city,
> Ring-a-ling, hear them ring,
> Soon it will be Christmas day.

10. *The Christmas Waltz*
Music and lyrics by Sammy Cahn and Julie Styne
Sung by Frank Sinatra

CHAPTER 13

Valentine's Day

History

Valentine's Day and its traditions originated in two separate Roman feasts:

Lupercalia

Feast Day of Juno Febrata

Lupercalia

St. Valentine's Day can be traced back to Lupercalia, the Roman "festival of sexual license." This purification and fertility festival seems to have been uniquely Roman... "There is no other indo-European equivalent in Vedic, Irish, Scandinavian, or indo-Iranian traditions." It origin has been lost to us, although it might have been associated with protection from wolves (lupus in Latin).

Even the pagan priests, called Luperci, had only a single function: to conduct the Lupercalia Festival annually on February 15. Cicero described them as: "... a certain wild association of Lupercalia brothers, both plainly pastoral and savage, whose rustic alliance was formed before civilization and laws ... (cael. 26)

The celebration was held in the Lupercalia cave on Palantine Hill in Rome. Here, it was believed, Romulus and Remus had been sheltered and fed by a she-wolf before they founded Rome. Two naked young priests, assisted by Vestal Virgins, would sacrifice a dog and a goat. The priests then clothed themselves with loincloths made from the skins of the goat. They ran about the city, scourging (flog, beat, whip, lash, strap, belt, torment, curse, afflict, using leather, plague, etc. Webster's Dictionary) women with februa (Latin for "means of purification"). These were strips of skin taken from the sacrifice goat. The Romans believed that this flogging would purify them, and assure their future fertility and easy childbirth. Feasts and parties were later celebrated throughout the city.

Juno Februata

The month of February was sacred to "Juno Februata, the goddess of the "fever" (febris in Latin) of love" in ancient pagan Rome. She was also the goddess of women and of marriage. February 14 was her festival day. At that time, a box was provided from which single men could draw a "billet," a small piece of paper on which a woman's name was written. The couple would then form a temporary liaison (mediator) for the erotic games (sexually arousing, excitement, desire, stimulating, titillating) to follow. They would remain partners for the following 12 months. Sometime marriages resulted from this practice.

The church was opposed to this display of open eroticism and sensuality. They tried various ways of changing the festivals. One method was to replace the woman's name with those of saints and short sermons. The young women and men were expected to emulate the life of the saint whose name was on the billet that they had drawn. However, it was soon apparent that the public preferred the old ways. By the 14th century, they once again tried to have saintly valentines, but it was as unsuccessful as the first time.

Cupid

Cupid in Roman mythology was the same god as Amor or Eros in ancient Greece. He was a minor god, the son of Venus, the Roman goddess of love and beauty. Eros seemed to be a cute, chubby cherub with bow and arrow, ready to shoot people and was responsible for impregnating a number of goddesses and mortals.

The ancient Greeks believed Eros was the force, "love," a force they believed was behind all creation. He is portrayed today as he infects them with pangs of love. He is often associated with Valentine's Day. The name, Cupid, is from the Latin verb, cupere, meaning, "to desire." The word valentine comes from the Latin, "valentinus," which derives from "valens," to be strong, powerful, and mighty.

The Heart Symbol

In ancient Chaldean (the language of the Babylonians), Bal, which is similar to Baal, meant, "heart." This is where the valentine heart symbol originated. The title, Baal, means "lord or master," and is mentioned throughout the Bible as the god of pagans.

In A.D. 494, Pope Gelasius renamed the festival of Juno Februata as the "Feast of the Purification of the Virgin Mary." The date of its observance was later changed from February 14 to February 2, then changed back to the 14th. It is also known as Candlemas, the Presentation of the Lord, the Purification of the Blessed Virgin, and the Feast of the Presentation of Christ in the temple. After Constantine had made the Roman church's brand of Christianity the official religion of the Roman Empire (A.D. 325), church leaders wanted to do away with the pagan festivals of the people. According to the Catholic Encyclopedia," at least three different Saint Valentine's, all of them martyrs, are mentioned in early martyrologies under the date of 14 February. One is described as a priest at Rome, another as bishop of Interamna (modern Terni), and these two seem both to have suffered in the second half of the third century and to have been buried on the Flaminian Way, but at different distances from the city. Of the third Saint Valentine, who suffered in Africa with a number of companions, nothing is further known. Several biographies of different men named valentine were merged into one "official" St. Valentine.

Valentine's Day by the Numbers

The holiday, once marked by amorous missives and hand-plucked posies, has evolved into a day of staggering statistics. From a dark history, Saint Valentine's Day emerged as a much sweeter holiday in the middle ages and became a popular occasion to celebrate romance. Handmade cards and billets-doux were the currency of love—eventually flowers were introduced into the fray.

The 19th century ushered in factory-made cards and 1913 brought us Hallmark Cards of Kansas City, Missouri. And just like that, Valentine's Day has never been the same. While retailers and manufactures of heart-shaped schmaltz surely appreciate our conflation of love and consumerism, it's hard not feel a bit dirty in a good way.

Not to be a cynic or anything, but we spend a lot of money and create a lot of waste on Valentine's Day and that doesn't feel very lovely. Here's the breakdown for sweethearts in the United States, according to the National Retail Federation's Valentine's Day consumer spending survey:

1. 91 - Percentage of people who plan to treat their significant others to something special for the heart-themed day

2. 58.7 - Percentage of people who will purchase gifts for other family members and for children's classmate and teachers

One quarter - Number of Valentine's revelers who will

shop online

13.3 - Percentage who will shop at a local or small business to find something special

703 million: Amount of money that will be spent on pets

$1.5 billion - Amount that will be spent on gift cards (because nothing says "I love you" like, "I have no clue what to get you)

$1.7 billion - Amount that will be spent on candy

$2 billion - Amount that will be spent on clothing

$2.1 billion - Amount that will be spent on flowers

$3.6 billion - Amount that will be spent on a special night out

$4.8 billion - Amount that will be spent on jewelry

$18.9 billion - Total amount Americans are expected to spend on Valentine's Day this year

$66 million - TOTAL number of hungry school-age children across the globe who could be fed for six years for the same amount of money Americans will spend on Valentine's Day this year

Seriously, if any of the Valentines could awake from their graves, would they approve all this foolishness over their names? No wonder why America is so broke. Instead of putting our money to good use, we find things to spend on that really count for nothing the next day, or even the next year.

When my children were young, we liked to do arts and crafts, making homemade cards were so much fun to make together. I would draw characters on paper, my sons used to color them, I would help them cut them out and paste them onto construction paper, and write to my friend on them. There are all kinds of ways to make cards—if you have a creative mind, that is. And by being creative, you will draw closer to your child.

Flowers Symbols

1. Roses —*Love, romance, beauty, perfection*
2. Gerbera Daisies —*Beauty, purity, innocence*
3. Tulips —*Perfect love, comfort, warmth*
4. Alstroemeria-peruvian lilies—*Friendship, devotion*
5. Casa blanca lilies —Beauty, class, style
6. Orchids —*Love, beauty, luxury, and strength*
7. Carnations —*New love, fascination*
8. Sunflowers —*Warmth, happiness, loyalty*
9. Iris —*Royalty, faith, and hope*
10. Gardenias —*Purity, joy, old-fashioned love*
11. Succulents —*Aloe, cacti, spiny than delicate*

Melissa Breyer. Economics. January 29, 2015.

CHAPTER 14

Birthdays

Biblical Background

Is birthday keeping biblical? Does God agree with this practice? Many Christians around the world do not realize that they are doing wrong, for they have never been taught any different—not even by a minister.

Believe it or not, but God has given you a manual—the Bible! God does not want His people to be blind to His word. God's expressed will and purpose is written throughout the pages. Every word of Scripture is His message to you—who you are in Him, what you are, why He created you, and how He expects you to conduct your life. Everything you need to know about the purpose of life is written in the Word of God. (Matt. 4:4; 2 Tim. 3:16-17; John 17:17)

Birthdays are mentioned in the Bible on three separate occasions and, in each case, something terrible had happened. These three accounts bear brief examination.

The first account is in Genesis. Pharaoh, the Egyptian king, celebrated his birthday by executing his chief baker

(Gen.40:1-23). God gave Joseph special understanding of a dream by Pharaoh's butler and baker, that the baker would lose his life three days after Joseph interpreted the dream. Joseph understood that Pharaoh would use this occasion—his own birthday party—to put his baker to death. As the dream had foretold, the baker was hung at the party.

The second account is found in the book of Job. The Bible says that Job's seven sons "went and feasted in their homes, every one his day, and sent and called for their sisters to eat and to drink with them" (Job1:4). These parties were obviously not centered around any kind of celebration related to God, or Job would not have worried that his children may have sinned during these celebration feasts. He was not exactly sure what was going on in their minds, but the very celebration of their birthdays triggered great concern in him (1:5). Apparently, during the birthday party of Job's oldest son, God allowed Satan to kill all ten of Job's children through what appears to be a dust storm (Vs. 6-13, 1819).

Further proof that these birthday celebrations displeased God is found in Job 3. Take time to read the entire chapter carefully. Job spends much time cursing every aspect of the day of his birth. The loss of all his children, due to a birthday celebration, stunned and sobered him. His words make plain that there is nothing good about the day of a man's birth. Notice, he only cursed the day he was born.

In the third account, the New Testament figure, Herod the tetrarch, reluctantly ordered the beheading of John the Baptist (Jesus cousin, Matthew 14:3-11). Notice verse 6: "But when Herod's birthday was kept." During the dancing and merry-making at his birthday party, Herod got carried away and eventually made a promise that he did not want to keep. As a result, John the Baptist lost his head.

Some who are familiar with these accounts attempts to explain them away by saying that there is no statement contained within them that directly prohibits birthday celebrations. It is true that the previous Scriptures do not contain a direct condemnation of birthdays, starting with the phrase, "Thou shall not ... " or something similar.

But notice, every time someone had a birthday party in the Bible, something terrible happened. And so many times, even today in the news, you may hear of someone having a birthday party and things get out of hand and go wrong. Some may end up in jail, or dead.

I know many people around the world on their special day will send out invitations to give tribute to one's self. They will go to the mall and buy themselves new clothes for their special day or go to the beauty salon and get their nails done, or if you are a man, perhaps a shave. Go to the store to buy tons of food, order yourself the biggest cake that your pockets can afford or buy some beer perhaps, for you don't want to drink alone—what fun would that be?

Perhaps you will even get in the mood to decorate the

entire house and the back yard with balloons, trimmings, and lanterns or you will hire a caterer or slave all day in the kitchen to make everyone on your list happy that you had invited them to your special day. Get the old radio out and play your favorite jams or have the boys over for a bar-b-cue—nothing wrong with throwing a slab of ribs, chicken, hot-dogs, hamburger or deer, and elk meat on the old grill, and set around and talk about your wives to one another, or the weather, or who got a new truck, sports, when you had served in the military or whatever guys like to talk about. And then as each person shows up, you are expecting for them to bring to you a special gift or two, for it is your special day, isn't it? For it makes you feel good. I have heard someone spent $20,000, on his birthday, everybody dressed up like clowns, and others, if they can afford it, have the red carpet rolled out just for them, and tight security. Some people even have birthday parties that last more than a week, and cost over $100,000 dollars, for that special person wanted to make sure that his friends enjoyed themselves at his expense (nice, right?). I heard that some parties are on a private beach, where anything goes, including sex, dancing, drugs, smoking, drinking, and fireworks, (why not, it is one's own birthday, isn't it, and who knows, if you will wake up the next morning or not?) Some even will hire circus people to perform for them, and ride around on an elephant's back, and perform with the wild tigers, lions, and bears. Sounds like one awesome party!

And while you're at it, why not throw a masquerade party, hire a marching band, horse-drawn carriages, and let the theme be like Cinderella, and why not buy the biggest golden cake you can find and even buy an expensive ballroom gown, which you may not be able to afford. Spare no expense for your special day! Since it is your special day, and while you are at it, why won't you hire someone to serenade you.

The wildest birthday party that I have heard of only cost someone a million dollars. That tells me a few things about this person. Then, if that weren't enough, when the money went dry, he called a Brinks truck to bring him more money to spend, for he surely wanted to have a good time on his special day, and make all of his special friends feel happy.

Then I heard about a person who spent just three million dollars for his birthday party. If that weren't enough, why not give yourself a party all over the states and some countries as well. Party, party, party—what could be wrong with all this? There is an old saying that goes like this, as long as you got money, you will have plenty of friends, but once you are completely broke, no one wants you for their friend. And, in many cases, you will meet new relatives that you have no idea who they might be.

CHAPTER 15

Jewish Holidays

History

The date of Jewish holidays does not change from year to year. Holidays are celebrated on the same day of the Jewish calendar every year, but the Jewish year is not the same length as a solar year on the civil calendar used by most of the western world, where the date shifts.

Astronomical Phenomenas

The Jewish calendar is based on three astronomical phenomena:
1. Rotation of the earth about its axis (one day)
2. Revolution of the moon about the earth (one month)
3. Four revolutions of the earth about the sun (one year)

These three phenomena are independent of each other, so there is no direct correlation between them. On average, the moon revolves around the earth in about 29½ days.

The earth revolves around the sun in about 365¼ days, that is, about 12.4 lunar months. The civil calendar used by most of the world has abandoned any correlation between the moon cycles and the month, arbitrarily setting the length of months to 28, 30, or 31 days. The Jewish calendar, however, coordinates all three of these astronomical phenomena.

Months are either 29 or 30 days, corresponding to the 29½-day lunar cycle. Years are either 12 or 13 months, corresponding to the 12.4 month solar cycle. The lunar month on the Jewish calendar begins when the first sliver of moon becomes visible after the dark of the moon.

In ancient times, the new months were determined by observation. When people saw the new moon, they would notify the Sanhedrin. When they heard testimony from two independent, reliable eyewitnesses that the new moon occurred on a certain date, they would declare the Rosh Chodesh (1st of the month) and send out messengers to tell people when the month began

The problem with strictly lunar calendars is that there are approximately 12.4 lunar months in every solar year, so a 12-month lunar calendar is about 11 days shorter than a solar year and a 13-month lunar is about 19 days longer than a solar year.

The months drift around the seasons on such a calendar. On a 12-month lunar calendar, the month of Nissan, which is supposed to occur in the spring, would occur 11 days earlier in the season each year, eventually occurring in the winter, the fall, the summer, and then the spring again. On a 13-month lunar calendar, the same thing would happen in the other direction, and faster.

To compensate for this drift, the Jewish calendar uses a 12-month lunar calendar with an extra month occasionally added. The month of Nissan occurs 11 days earlier each year for two or three years, and then jumps forward 30 days, balancing out the drift.

In ancient times, this month was added by observation: the Sanhedrin observed the conditions of the weather, the crops and the livestock. If these were not sufficiently advanced to be considered "spring," they inserted an additional month into the calendar. This would ensure that Pesach (Passover) would occur in the spring—it is, after all, referred to in the Torah as Chag he-Aviv, the Festival of Spring!

A year with 13 months is referred to in Hebrew as Shanah me'uberet—literally, a pregnant year. In English, we commonly call it a leap year. The additional month is known as Adar I, Adar Rishon (first Adar) or Adar Alef (Hebrew letter alef being numeral "1" in Hebrew). The extra month is inserted before the regular month of Adar (known in such years as Adar II, Adar Sheini or Adar Beit).

Note that Adar II is the "real" Adar, the one in which Purim is celebrated, the one in which yahrzeits for Adar were observed, the one in which a 13-year-old born in Adar becomes a bar mitzvah. (bar, means son) Adar I is "extra" adar.

In the 4th century, Hillel II established a fixed calendar

based on mathematical and astronomical calculations. This calendar, still in use, standardized the length of months and the addition of months over the course of a 19-year cycle, so that the lunar calendar realigns with the solar years. Adar I is added in the 3rd, 6th ,8th , 11th ,14th ,17th and 19th years of the cycle. The current cycle began in Jewish calendar 5758).

If you are musically inclined, you may find it helpful to remember this pattern of leap years by reference to the major scale: for each whole step there are two regular years and a leap year; for each half-step there is one regular year and a leap year. In addition, Yom Kippur should not fall adjacent to Shabbat, because this would cause difficulties in coordinating the fast with Shabbat, and Hoshanah Rabbaah should not fall on Saturday, because it would interfere with the holiday observances. A day is added to the month of Cheshvan or subtracted from the month of Kislev of the previous year to prevent these things from happening. This process is sometimes referred to as "fixing" Rosh Hashanah. If you are interested in the details of how these calculations are performed, see the Jewish calendar: calculations of Jewish years.

The year number on the Jewish calendar represents the number of years since creation, calculated by adding up the ages of people in the Bible back to the time of creation. However, this does not necessarily mean that the universe has existed for only 5,700 years, as we understand years.

Many orthodox Jews will readily acknowledge that

the first six days of creation are not necessarily 24-hour days (indeed, a 24-hour day would be meaningless until the creation of the sun on the fourth "day"). For a fascinating (albeit) somewhat defensive) article by a nuclear physicist showing how Einstein's theory of relativity sheds light on the correspondence between the Torah's age of the universe and the age ascertained by science, see the "Age of the Universe.

Throughout my life, I have always wonder how exactly how "old" is this old earth, and the universe that is far above us. Some preachers say it is only about 3,000 years old, but scientists believe it is billions of years old.

Does anyone know the truth except God himself? Many people say there is no way that God could have created the entire world in six days, and rested on the Sabbath. Mankind complains all the time, saying there are never enough hours in a day. Will they never to happy? God as gave man life. Ever since man was created by God, he has been trying to figure God out. Some say that God is a great mystery. Man has learned many false teachings in so many generations, instead of trusting in God who created him.

Instead of searching for the truth, ancient commentators purpose that the world may be simultaneously young and old. When we add up the generations of the Bible, we come to 5,700-plus years. Whereas, data from the Hubble telescope or from the land-based telescopes in Hawaii indicate the age at about 15 billion years.

Since God is infinite, He could have made the universe

any which way he chose to do. The text of the Bible itself (3,300 years old), the translation of the Torah into Aramaic by Onkelos (100ce), the Talmud (redacted about the year 500ce), and the three major Torah commentators. There are many, many commentators, but at the very top of the mountain, there are three, accepted by all:

- Rashi (11th century France), who brings the straight understanding of the text

- Maimonides (12th century Egypt), who handles the philosophical concepts

- Nachmaides (13th century Spain), the earliest of the Kabbalists

This ancient commentary was finished long before Hubble was a gleam in his great-grandparent's eye, so there's no possibility of Hubbel or any other modern scientific data influencing these concepts.

In 1959, astronomy was popular, but cosmology—the deep physics of understanding the universe—was just being birthed. Many scientists believed there was never a "beginning." They accept what Plato and Aristotle taught them 2400 years ago that the universe is eternal. They said, "Oh, we know what the Bible says—in the beginning. That's a nice story, but we sophisticates know better. There was no beginning."

Notice this: Penzias and Wilson discovered the echo of the big bang in the black of the sky at night, and the world paradigm changed from a universe that was eternal to a universe that had a beginning. After 3,000 years of arguing, science has come to agree finally with the word of God.

Jews do not generally use the terms, "A.D." and "B.C.," to refer to the years on the civil calendar. Because "A.D." means" the year of our lord," and many Jews today yet still do not recognize Jesus as the Messiah of the world prophesied in the Old Testament. My friend considers him as a rabbi-teacher who walked once among the Jews, and the Gentiles.

The Jewish people instead use the abbreviation c.e. (common or Christian era) which are commonly used by scholars today.

Months of the Jewish Calendar

The first month of the Jewish calendar is Nissan, in the spring, when Passover occurs. However, the Jewish New Year is in Tishri, the seventh month, and that is when the year number is increased.

This concept of different starting points for a year is not as strange as it might seem at first glance. Americans New Year starts on the first day of January each year, but the new school year starts in September.

The names of the months of the Jewish calendar were adopted during the time of Ezra, after the return from the Babylonian exile (598/7bce, reign of Jehoiachin, who reigned three months). The names are actually Babylonian month names, brought back to Israel by the returning exiles. The Bible refers to months by numbers, not by name. Here are the names of the months in the Jewish calendar in English:

Name	Length	Civil Equivalent
1 Nissan	30 days	Mar-April
2 Iyar	29days	April-May
3 Sivan	30 days	May-June
4 Tammuz	29 days	June-July
5 Av	30 days	July-Aug
6 Elul	29 days	Aug-Sept
7 Tishri	30 days	Sept-Oct
8 Cheshran	29 or 30 days	Oct-Nov
9 Kislev	30 or 29 days	Nov-Dec
10 Tevet	29 days	Dec-Jan
11 Shevat	30 days	Jan-Feb
12 Adar I	30 days	Feb-Mar
12 (13 in leap years) Adar (called adar beit in leap year)	29 days	Feb-Mar

The length of Cheshvan and Kislev are determined by complex calculations involving the time of day of the full moon of the following year's Tishri and the day of the week that Tishri would occur in the following year. The number of days between Nissan and Tishri is always the same. Because of this, the time from the first major festival (Passover) in Nissan to the last major festival (Sukkot in Tishri) is always the same.

Other than Sabbath, the name of the seventh day of

the week on the Jewish calendar doesn't have names for the days of the week. The days of the week are simply known as the first day, second day, third day, etc. Sometimes they are referred to more fully as the first day of the sabbath. You may find out more information about the Jewish calendars on amazon.com.

http://www.jewfaq.org/calendar.htm

God's Law and Time vs. Man (Sabbath Day vs. Sunday)

Who did God give permission to change Sabbath keeping to Sunday keeping? This chapter contains some overwhelming facts that every Protestant needs to read. If the Protestant church of today knew what the Catholic church did in the past regarding the seventh day (Sabbath), they would not be worshipping on Sundays today—guaranteed!

If you are a true child of God seeking to do exactly as the Creator would have you do, the information in this chapter will affect you in a major way! Prophecy states plainly that the beast will seek to change "times and laws." This chapter includes ample evidence that the Roman Catholic Church admits to that very action.

The word of God says in Daniel 7:25, " ... and he shall speak great words against the most high, and shall wear out the saints of the most high, and think to change time and laws: and they shall be given into his hand until a time and times and the dividing of time."

The word of Rome says, "The pope has the power to change times, to abrogate laws, to abolish, do away, or annul, especially by authority. The pope has the power to change times, to abrogate laws, and to dispense with all things, even the precepts of Christ."

The pope has the authority and often exercised it, to dispense with the command of Christ. "Decretal, deTranlatic Episcop. Cap. (The pope can modify divine law.) Ferraris Ecclesiastical Dictionary. This is a copy of a calendar published by the Vatican showing the change made by Pope Gregory back in October of 1582.

Daniel's prophecy stated the beast would change "times" and "laws" and as many already know, the Vatican did, in fact, change the calendar in the past! Many of us are also aware that the Vatican changed the seventh day, Sabbath, to Sunday as well.

The prophecy of Daniel is 100% accurate on this point without a doubt! To illustrate this fact, here are a few facts for consideration.

Back in 1869, the Roman Catholic Church issued a letter that attacked Protestant believers for their desire to keep to the word of God. In this chapter, you will see for yourself how the Roman Catholic Church uses many bible verses to prove that Protestant churches are not doing as they should, if they truly want to be considered Bible-believing Christians. In essence, their main argument was regarding the seventh day, Sabbath, and that all Protestants were keeping a first day, Sabbath, according to Rome instead of the seventh day, Sabbath, according to Scriptures. The Vatican declared and historically proved that they are the ones that changed the Sabbath to Sunday—not the Bible-embracing Protestants who were still attending church on Sunday.

Anyway, so Rome's challenge was that if you claim to be Protestant, why is it you are keeping a doctrine that Rome itself can prove with 100% accuracy they invented without a single Bible passage as proof of that change? The Vatican was declaring that the Bible itself never allowed for the change, and they themselves had proof they made the change anyway, and Protestants the world over were doing as the Vatican suggested, over what the word of God commanded.

They "assumed" the Vatican must be above the Bible, because "all the world was wandering after the beast" and doing as Rome declared was doctrine. Are not Protestants bound by that which is written? Are they not bound to "obey God rather than man, according to Acts 5:29? Yet since we have historic proof, as well as modern day reality, we see the Protestants aren't really protesting at all. They are doing as Rome suggests over and above that which the word of God commands.

It appeared the Vatican has a case. Of course, the main issue of this challenge was to try and convert the Protestants into thinking as does the Catholic and, therefore, realize they may as well return to Rome. They wanted them to realize that the Bible is not the "sole authority" and therefore is not worthy of a trustworthy embrace.

The Vatican thought they had "proof" the Protestants believed as they did regarding sola scriptura. The Vatican was hoping to use this letter to convince the masses that the Catholic Church must be the true church, because all Protestants were doing as they suggested in regards to Sunday-keeping.

This letter, as well as a series of articles that appeared in the Catholic Mirror, which by the way, was an official "organ" of Cardinal Gibbons back in 1893, caused many to return to Rome as their home. However, the wonderful irony of this whole thing is that it backfired in their faces, as well.

This ministry alone has seen many people come to know the truth about the Sabbath by merely sharing with them this admission of Rome that they are indeed the ones that thought they could change times and laws, as Daniel prophesied the Beast of Rome would do if the shield of Pope Gregory as it is displayed in the Vatican.

Notice the "dragon" is his depiction. Here is a letter from the Roman Catholic Church originally published in America in 1869. The message was written to protestants and is forceful and to the point, with lots of scriptural proof for its position.

Here is a very plain and serious question for those who follow "the Bible and the Bible only" to give their most earnest attention: why do you not keep holy the Sabbath

Day? The commands of almighty God stands clearly written in the Bible in these words, Remember the Sabbath Day, to keep it holy. Six days shalt thou labor, and do all thy work, but the seventh day is the sabbath of the lord thy god; in it thou shalt not do any work (Ex. 20:8-10).

And again, "Six days shall work be done; but on the seventh day there shall be unto you an holy day, a sabbath of rest to the lord, whosoever doeth work therein shall be put to death" (Ex. 2, 3). God made the Sabbath. He rested on it. He sanctified it and set it apart from all the rest of the days. He blessed it and He made it to be the seventh day of a seven-day cycle.

If this cycle has been either broken or lost, there remains no further obligation for mankind to observe the true Sabbath that God designed in the beginning (Gen. 2:1). It is that simple. If the weekly cycle has been broken, the Sabbath is lost to history and cannot be in effect today.

Keeping Track of the Sabbath

One day I was talking with a friend of mine. We were trying to figure out our weekly schedules together. When I mentioned that the Sabbath falls on October 31 this year, she became confused, thinking I meant Sunday (the first day of the week). Even Sunday school teachers will misinform children to thinking that Sunday is the Lord's day known as the Sabbath. One of God's commandments bids us to keep it holy, and yet they are teaching a lie, being deceived by the devil. Many people today know not what the true Sabbath is, for they are confused, because they have been taught this as little children.

The truth is staring at them into their own faces, yet they can't seem to see it as what it is, for they have been taught differently. Do you not think for one minute the all-powerful God of the universe is capable of creating, hallowing, sanctifying, and blessing the seventh day of the week, yet at the same time, incapable of keeping track of this day throughout history? Would God command people to "remember" the Sabbath, only to forget that He must preserve it for this to be possible?

The idea is absurd. It insults God's power by making Him appear to be an old forgetful man sitting on a cloud watching a huge clock passing the time away. Or perhaps He is so disorganized and forgetful that He cannot keep track of what He has created or commanded!

While mankind seeks excuses not to keep the Sabbath, some actually dare to blame God is the reason this is no longer possible, then reasoning that if He forgot to preserve the weekly cycle, mankind no longer needs to observe the Sabbath. This world's professing Christianity—Catholicism and the many other branches of Protestantism—keep Sunday. It has been the Roman Catholic Church that has preserved Sunday as the day of worship.

Notice the following stunning admission from a letter by James Cardinal Gibbons, Archbishop of Baltimore (1877-1921), while it also makes a statement about how

Sabbath obedience was exchanged for Sunday observance, this quote demonstrates the importance of the preservation of Sunday observance for Catholics throughout the centuries. This is only one of many similar quotes:

> Is Saturday the seventh day according to the Bible and the Ten Commandments? I answer yes. Is Sunday the first day of the week? And did the church (Roman Catholic) change the seventh day—Saturday—for Sunday, the first day? I answer yes. Did Christ change the day? I answer no.
>
> Faithfully your,
>
> J. Cardinal Gibbons.

No one ever seems to question that the first day of the week is Sunday. Two billion professing Christians assert that they keep Sunday in commemoration of Christ's supposed resurrection on that day—the first day of the week! It is unthinkable to suggest that so many people would either purposely, carelessly, or traditionally be keeping this day, the first day of the week, Sunday, on the wrong day! Right? But Jews are no less certain that they are keeping the Sabbath on the true seventh day of the week. The Jewish people have been responsible for "keeping track" of their day, the same day kept by Jesus and the apostles, for many centuries longer than Catholics have been tracking" the day.

The point is this: each group (Catholics and Jews)

knows full well which day is which—and neither would dare suggest the other does not!

The Manna Miracle

It has been established that God gave the Sabbath to ancient Israel though Moses. Why did He do this? He had to! Israel had just spent near 250 years me Egypt, with most of that time in slavery. They had not been permitted to worship the one true God of their forefathers, Abraham, Isaac, and Jacob, for all those years. At the time that God liberated them, they had forgotten the identity of their almighty God and his true Sabbath. This is the one reason that the Sabbath command begins with the words, "Remember the Sabbath Day"—Israel had forgotten it.

Abraham, Isaac, and Jacob had kept God's law (Gen. 26:5), but the knowledge of the Sabbath had become lost through the centuries. God decided to make the Sabbath command clear to Israel while they were in the Wilderness of Sin (Zin). Moses, having succeeded in bringing the Jews out of Egypt, while consequently and repeatedly being confronted by angry hordes of newly liberated Jews incessantly complaining about the harshness of life in the expansive deserts where food and water were scarce. Exodus 16:3 refers to one such collective lament directed at Moses by angry throngs: "Would to God we had died by the hand of the lord in the land of Egypt, where we sat by the flesh-pots, and when we did eat bread to the full; for ye have brought us forth into this wilderness, to kill his whole assembly with hunger."

The test had begun—would Israel keep God's law—keep His Sabbath? Would they walk in His law or not? The context continues, " … and Moses spoke unto Aaron, say unto all the congregation of the children of Israel, come near before the lord: for he has heard your murmurings. And it came to pass, as Aaron spoke unto the whole congregation of the children of Israel, that they looked toward the wilderness, and, behold, the glory of the Lord appeared in the cloud … And it came to pass, that at even, the quails came and covered the camp and in the morning the dew lay round about the host." (vs. 9-13)

It is important to realize that the quail did not come up until after sunset. Also, Israel was assembled as a whole on the Sabbath day. They were gathered for a religious service. The quails appeared when the Sabbath was over, and people were permitted to gather them for the evening meal. The next morning was the last day of the week and this time when manna appeared, the people were instructed to only gather enough for each day, or it would breed worms and stink (vs. 20). The people disbelieved Moses and attempted to gather extra manna. Just as God said, it bred worms and stank. However, verse 22 explains that on the sixth day of the week they could gather twice as much, so they would have food for the Sabbath, and it would not breed worms and stink.

God said this because "tomorrow is the rest of the holy

Sabbath unto the lord" (vs. 23). As is always the case, some did not believe God and attempted to gather manna on the Sabbath—the seventh day (vs. 27). Just as God had said, they found none. How quickly some became confused about time! These Israelites must have thought "time had been lost" and that the manna would be there even though God had told them it would not. God's response to those who became confused was: "How long will ye refuse to keep my commandments and my laws?"